Fast Track Certified Java Programmer (SCJP) 5.0 Upgrade Exam

Copyright © 2006

Ka Iok 'Kent' Tong

Publisher:	TipTec Development
Author's email:	freemant2000@yahoo.com
Book website:	http://www.agileskills2.org
Notice:	All rights reserved. No part of this publication may be reproduced, stored in a retrieval system or transmitted, in any form or by any means, electronic, mechanical, photocopying, recording, or otherwise, without the prior written permission of the publisher.
ISBN:	978-1-4303-0393-0
Edition:	First edition 2006

Foreword

Learn the new features in Java SE 5.0

If you'd like to learn the new features in Java SE 5.0 and pass the Sun Certified Java Programmer Upgrade Exam (CX-310-056), then this book is for you. Why?

- It covers all the Java SE 5.0 new features covered in the exam. You don't need to read about the features you already know.

- It is clear & concise. No need to go through hundreds of pages.

- I have passed the exam. So I know what you'll be up against.

- It includes 117 review questions and mock exam questions.

- Many working code fragments are used to show the semantics of the code construct concerned.

- The first 30 pages are freely available on http://www.agileskills2.org. You can judge it yourself.

Target audience and prerequisites

This book is suitable for those who would like to:

- Learn the new features in Java SE 5.0; or

- Take the Sun Certified Java Programmer Upgrade Exam.

In order to understand what's in the book, you need to know the basics of Java. In order to take the exam, you also need to have passed a previous version of the exam.

Acknowledgments

I'd like to thank:

- Helena Lei for proofreading this book.

- Eugenia Chan Peng U for doing the book cover and the layout design.

Table of Contents

Chapter 1

Autoboxing

What's in this chapter?

In this chapter you'll learn about autoboxing.

Autoboxing

In J2SE 1.4 or earlier, you can't directly add say an int to a collection because it needs an Object. You need to wrap it into an Integer object:

```
List list = new ArrayList();
list.add(100); //error: 100 is not an Object
list.add(new Integer(100)); //OK
```

This action of wrapping is called "boxing". In JSE 5.0, whenever the compiler sees that you're trying to assign a primitive value to a variable of a reference type, it will automatically insert the code to convert the primitive value into a wrapper object for you (int => Integer, long => Long, float => Float, double => Double, etc.):

```
List list = new ArrayList();
list.add(100);
```

This is OK in JSE 5.0. The compiler may turn this line into:

```
list.add(new Integer(100));
```

This is called "autoboxing". It not only works for collections, but also for all kinds of assignments:

```
Integer i = 100; //OK
Integer[] a = new Integer[] { new Integer(2), 4, 1, 3}; //OK
g(100);
...
void g(Integer i) {
  ...
}
```

Because it is valid to have:

```
byte b;
b = 100; //100 is an int but it's a constant & within the scope of a byte,
         //so it's converted to a byte.
```

JSE 5.0 will also allow:

```
Byte b;
b = 100; //converted to a byte and then to a Byte (autoboxing)
Byte[] bs = new Byte[] {100, -128, 127}; //do that for each element
```

Auto unboxing

The reverse also works: If you'd like to assign say an Integer object to an int variable, it will be "unboxed" automatically:

```
int i = new Integer(100); //OK
Integer[] a = new Integer[] { new Integer(2), new Integer(5) };
```

```
int j = a[0]; //OK
List list = new ArrayList();
list.add(new Integer(10));
int k = (Integer)list.get(0); //OK
```

Other contexts

Autoboxing and auto unboxing occur not only in assignments, but also in other contexts where the conversion is clearly desired. For example, in an if-statement:

```
if (Boolean.TRUE) { //OK
  ...
}
```

In an arithmetic expression:

```
int i = 10+new Integer(2)*3; //i is 16
Integer j = 10;
j++; //j is 11
```

In a logical expression:

```
if (new Integer(2) > 1) { //OK
  ...
}
```

In a casting:

```
((Integer)100).hashCode(); //OK
((Short)100).hashCode(); //Error: Short is not the right wrapper
```

Autoboxing and method name overloading

Check the code below:

```
class Foo {
  void g(int x) {
    System.out.println("a");
  }
  void g(long x) {
    System.out.println("b");
  }
  void g(Integer x) {
    System.out.println("c");
  }
}
...
new Foo().g(10);
```

What will it print? It will print "a". When the compiler is trying to determine which method it is calling, it will first ignore autoboxing and unboxing. So the first two g() methods are applicable but the third g() is inapplicable. Because the first g() is more specific than the second, it is used. If there were no applicable method, then it would allow autoboxing and unboxing. For example, if the code were:

```
class Foo {
  void g(byte x) {
    System.out.println("a");
  }
  void g(char x) {
    System.out.println("b");
```

```
    }
  void g(Integer x) {
    System.out.println("c");
  }
}
...
new Foo().g(10);
```

Then the first two g() methods would be inapplicable because byte and char are narrower than int (the type of the value 10). Then it would proceed to allow autoboxing and find that the third g() would be applicable, so it would be called and would print "c".

Summary

Autoboxing converts an primitive value to a wrapper object. Auto unboxing does the opposite. They work in assignments and other contexts where the conversion is clearly desired.

When finding applicable methods, autoboxing and unboxing are first disabled, so existing code will not be affected by them. If there is no applicable method, they will be enabled to allow more methods.

Review questions

1. Will the following code compile?

```
boolean b = Boolean.TRUE;
if (b) {
  ...
}
```

2. Will the following code compile?

```
if (Boolean.TRUE) {
  ...
}
```

3. Will the following code compile?

```
((Boolean)true).hashCode();
```

4. Will the following code compile?

```
Object[] a = new Object[] { 'a', true, 10.0d, 123, "xyz" };
```

5. What is the output of the following code?

```
public class Foo {
  void g(double d) {
    System.out.println("d");
  }
  void g(Number num) {
    System.out.println("num");
  }
  void g(Object obj) {
    System.out.println("obj");
  }
  public static void main(String[] args) {
    new Foo().g(10);
    new Foo().g(new Integer(10));
  }
}
```

Answers to review questions

1. Will the following code compile?

```
boolean b = Boolean.TRUE;
if (b) {
  ...
}
```

Yes. Autoboxing occurs in the assignment.

2. Will the following code compile?

```
if (new Integer(10)==10) {
  ...
}
```

Yes. Autoboxing occurs in the logical expression.

3. Will the following code compile?

```
((Boolean)true).hashCode();
```

Yes. Autoboxing occurs in a type cast.

4. Will the following code compile?

```
Object[] a = new Object[] { 'a', true, 10.0d, 123, "xyz" };
```

Yes. Autoboxing works for a char, a boolean, a double, an int. For "xyz" there is no autoboxing needed.

5. What is the output of the following code?

```
public class Foo {
  void g(double d) {
    System.out.println("d");
  }
  void g(Number num) {
    System.out.println("num");
  }
  void g(Object obj) {
    System.out.println("obj");
  }
  public static void main(String[] args) {
    new Foo().g(10);
    new Foo().g(new Integer(10));
  }
}
```

For the first call, it will print "d". Because double is wider than int, so the first g () is applicable. At the beginning, autoboxing and unboxing are not considered, so the second and third g() are not applicable. So the first g() is the only applicable method and thus is used.

For the second call, at the beginning autoboxing and unboxing are not considered, so the first g() is inapplicable but the second and third g() methods are. Because the second is more specific than the third, it is used.

Mock exam

1. What is true about the following code?

```
1.  short s1 = 100;
2.  Short s2 = s1;
3.  Integer i = s1;
```

   a. There is a compile error at line 1.

   b. There is a compile error at line 2.

   c. There is a compile error at line 3.

   d. It will compile fine.

2. What is true about the following code?

```
1.  Integer i = 10;
2.  int j = 5;
3.  if (i.compareTo(j) > 0) {
4.    System.out.println("OK");
5.  }
```

   a. It will print "OK".

   b. It will print nothing.

   c. There is a compile error at line 2.

   d. There is a compile error at line 3.

3. What is true about the following code?

```
1.  int i = 10;
2.  Integer j = 5;
3.  if (i.compareTo(j) > 0) {
4.    System.out.println("OK");
5.  }
```

   a. It will print "OK".

   b. It will print nothing.

   c. There is a compile error at line 2.

   d. There is a compile error at line 3.

4. What is true about the following code?

```
1.  class Foo {
2.    void g(int i) {
3.      System.out.println("a");
4.    }
5.  }
6.  class Bar extends Foo {
7.    void g(Integer i) {
8.      System.out.println("b");
9.    }
10. }
11. ...
12. Bar b = new Bar();
13. b.g(10);
```

   a. It will print "a".

b. It will print "b".

c. It will print "ab".

d. It won't compile because the g() in Bar can't override the g() in Foo.

Answers to the mock exam

1. c. Autoboxing will convert a short to a Short, but not to an Integer.

2. a. "j" will be converted to an Integer automatically when it is passed to compareTo().

3. d. "i" will not be converted to an Integer automatically because there is no assignment nor casting there.

4. a. The g() in Bar is not overriding the g() in Foo. It is just overloading the name "g". When determining which method to call, autoboxing is not considered first so only the g() in Foo is applicable and thus is used.

Chapter 2

Generics

What's in this chapter?

In this chapter you'll learn how to use generics and how to create your own.

Using generics

In J2SE 1.4 or earlier, the collection types were like:

```
interface Collection {
  void add(Object obj);
}
interface List extends Collection {
  Object get(int idx);
}
class ArrayList implements List {
  ...
}
```

In JSE 5.0, they have been changed to:

```
interface Collection<E> {
  void add(E obj);
}
interface List<E> extends Collection<E> {
  E get(int idx);
}
class ArrayList<E> implements List<E> {
  ...
}
```

The "E" represents the type of the element of the collection. It is called a "type parameter". When you use them, you need to specify a type as the actual value of E:

```
List<String> list = new ArrayList<String>(); //It reads "a List of Strings"
```

You can imagine that the compiler will generate code like:

```
interface Collection<String> {
  void add(String obj); //can only add String
}
interface List<String> extends Collection<String> {
  String get(int idx); //will return a String
}
class ArrayList<String> implements List<String> {
  ...
}
```

It means that you can call add() and pass a String object but not other types of objects. When you call get(), it will return a String, not an Object:

```
list.add("hello"); //OK
list.add(new Integer(10)); //Error! In J2SE 1.4 it would be OK
String s = list.get(0); //No need to type cast to String anymore
```

The Collection and List interfaces are called "generic interfaces". The ArrayList class is a "generic class". When you provide a type argument, the resulting types such as List<String> or ArrayList<String> are called "parameterized types", while the original types (List, ArrayList) are called "raw types". The act of providing a type argument is called "invocation".

Similarly, the Set interface and its implementation classes are also generic:

```
Set<Integer> set = new TreeSet<Integer>(); //Integer implements Comparable
set.add(new Integer(2));
set.add(5); //OK. Autoboxing.
set.add("hello"); //Error!
if (set.contains(2)) { //It will be true
   ...
}
```

So are Map and its implementation classes:

```
//It has two type parameters
interface Map<K,V> {
  void put(K key, V value);
}
...
//Key is an Integer. Value is a String. Integer implements hashCode().
Map<Integer, String> map = new HashMap<Integer, String>();
map.put(3, "a");
map.put(5, "b");
map.put(4, 2); //Error!
map.put("c", 2); //Error!
String s = map.get(5); //It is "b"
```

Now, the Iterator interface is also generic:

```
interface Collection<E> {
  Iterator<E> iterator();
  ...
}
interface Iterator<E> {
  boolean hasNext();
  E next();
}
```

Therefore, you can iterate a list like this:

```
List<String> list = new ArrayList<String>(); //a List of Strings
list.add("a");
list.add("b");
for (Iterator<String> iter = list.iterator(); iter.hasNext(); ) {
  String s = iter.next(); //No need to type cast
  System.out.println(s);
}
```

Parameterized types are compile-time properties of variables

Consider the code:

```
List<String> list1 = new ArrayList<String>();
List<Integer> list2 = new ArrayList<Integer>();
list1 = list2; //Error
list2 = list1; //Error
if (list1.getClass()==list2.getClass()) { //It will be true!
   ...
}
```

It means the two List objects actually belong to the same class! This is true. When the compiler sees the List interface, it will remove E and change it into Object and use the result as the runtime class (called the "erasure" of the generic class):

```
interface Collection {
  void add(Object obj);
}
interface List extends Collection {
```

```
    Object get(int idx);
}
class ArrayList implements List {
    ...
}
```

When you invoke it like this:

```
List<String> list1 = new ArrayList<String>();
```

The compiler will note that the type of the variable list1 is List with the binding of E=String. Later, suppose that there is some code calling add() on list1:

```
list1.add(...);
```

The compiler knows that the type of list1 is List. So it checks the definition of Collection, it finds that the parameter's type of add() is E:

```
interface Collection<E> {
    void add(E obj);
}
interface List<E> extends Collection<E> {
    E get(int idx);
}
```

From the binding in list1, it notes that E=String, so it will check to make sure the method argument is assignment compatible with String. If it is say an Integer, then the compiler will treat it as an error.

Similarly, if you call get() on list1:

```
String s = list1.get(0);
```

From the definition of Collection, the compiler finds that the return type of get() is E. From the binding in list1 it notes that E=String, so it will insert some code to type cast the result to a String:

```
String s = (String)list1.get(0);
```

That is how generic works. The code we imagined before:

```
interface Collection<String> {
    void add(String obj); //can only add String
}
interface List<String> extends Collection<String> {
    String get(int idx); //will return a String
}
class ArrayList<String> implements List<String> {
    ...
}
```

is never generated. At runtime only the raw types exist. The type bindings are properties of variables at compile-time only. They are used during compilation for type checking (as for add()) or to generate type cast code (as for get()). At runtime, the type bindings and the parameterized types no longer exist. Because the "new" operator runs at runtime, new'ing a parameterized type really doesn't make sense:

```
List<String> list = new ArrayList<String>();
```

So, at runtime, what it does is exactly the same as:

```
List<String> list = new ArrayList();
```

However, at compile-time, the <String> is indeed required so that the compiler knows that the type of the expression is ArrayList<String>.

As another example, let's write a class Pair to represent a pair of objects of the same type. You may try:

```
class Pair<E> {
  E obj1; //Compiled as "Object obj1". Doesn't affect anything at runtime.
  E obj2; //Compiled as "Object obj2". Doesn't affect anything at runtime.

  Pair() {
    obj1 = new E(); //Compiled as "new Object()". Affects runtime. Error.
    obj2 = new E(); //Compiled as "new Object()". Affects runtime. Error.
  }
  void setObj1(E o) { //Compiled as "Object o". Doesn't affect runtime.
    obj1 = o;
  }
}
```

Assignment compatibility between parameterized type variables

Obviously the code below won't compile:

```
List<String> list1 = new ArrayList<String>();
List<Integer> list2 = new ArrayList<Integer>();
list1 = list2; //Compile error
list2 = list1; //Compile error
```

But what about:

```
class Animal {
}
class Dog extends Animal {
}
...
List<Animal> list1 = new ArrayList<Animal>();
List<Dog> list2 = new ArrayList<Dog>();
list1 = list2; //OK?
```

Intuitively, a List of Dog should be a List of Animal. But this is not the case here:

```
List<Animal> list1 = new ArrayList<Animal>();
List<Dog> list2 = new ArrayList<Dog>();
list1 = list2; //OK? No!
list1.add(new Animal());
Dog d = list2.get(0); //Runtime error!
```

For list1, the binding is E=Animal. It means the object it points to can accept any Animal object through its add() method (see the diagram below). For list2, the binding is E=Dog. It means the object it points to can accept any Dog object through its add() method. Obviously we can't just let list1 point to the object pointed to by list2 because that object doesn't accept any Animals, but just Dogs. Our intuition would be correct if the list objects were read-only (e.g., only had a get() method).

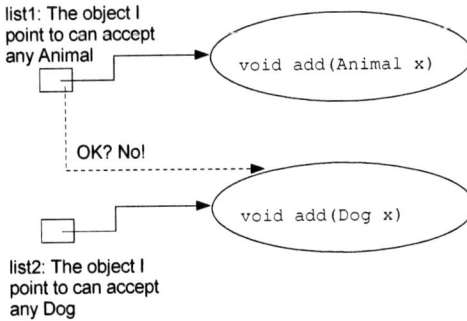

list1: The object I
point to can accept
any Animal

void add(Animal x)

OK? No!

void add(Dog x)

list2: The object I
point to can accept
any Dog

Therefore, the Java compiler will consider two parameterized types of the same raw type completely unrelated at compile-time and are thus assignment incompatible.

Comparing a List to an array

See if the code below works:

Generic	Array
`List<Dog> dogs = new ArrayList<Dog>();` `List<Animal> animals = dogs;`	`Dog[] dogs = new Dog[10];` `Animal[] animals = dogs;`

As said before, the code on the left hand side won't compile. As a List of Dogs will accept only Dogs but not Animals, you can't assign a List<Dog> to a List<Animal>. But surprisingly, the array version on the right hand side works. It allows you to assign Bar[] to Foo[] if Bar is a subclass of Foo. It means it will allow dangerous code to compile:

```
Dog[] dogs = new Dog[10];
Animal[] animals = dogs; //Dangerous!
animals[0] = new Animal(); //Putting an Animal into a Dog array!
Dog d = dogs[0]; //It is not a Dog!
```

Why it allows such code to compile? Because it has very good runtime checking. When you create an array in Java, it remembers that its element type (e.g., the Dog array above knows its element type is Dog). When you try to put an object into its element, it will perform runtime checking to make sure it is a Dog:

```
Dog[] dogs = new Dog[10];
Animal[] animals = dogs;
animals[0] = new Animal(); //Runtime error
Dog d = dogs[0]; //Won't reach this line
```

Because generics only work at compile-time, they can't perform any runtime checking. Therefore, it takes a strict stance at compile time and forbids you to assign a List<Dog> to a List<Animal>. In contrast, arrays can rely on runtime checking, so it is more relaxed at compile time.

Now, check if the code below compiles:

```
class MyList<E> {
```

```
E[] objs; //Compiled as "Object[] objs". Doesn't affect runtime.
MyList() {
    E = new E[100]; //OK? No!
}
```

It won't compile. Because an array needs to know its element type when it is created at runtime, the element type must not be a type variable (which doesn't exist at runtime and has been compiled as the type "Object").

Similarly, you can't use a parameterized type as the element type of an array:

```
List<String>[] list; //OK
list = new List<String>[10]; //Compile error
```

Wildcard type

When you provide a type argument for a List, you may write something like:

```
List<?> list1;
```

The "?" represents a type that is unknown to the variable "list1". Such a type is called a "wildcard type". In this case, it is setting the binding E=? for variable "list1" where E is the type parameter in List. This means that list1 is asserting that the object it points to has an add() method that accepts an object of a certain type (unknown to list1) and a get() method that returns an object of a certain type (unknown to list1):

```
class List<?> {
    void add(? obj);
    ? get(int idx);
}
```

It means that we can't add any object to it because we don't know the right type:

```
List<?> list1;
list1.add("a"); //Compile error. It could accept only Integer.
list1.add(100); //Compile error. It could accept only String.
list1.add(new Object()); //Compile error. It could accept only Integer.
list1.add(null); //OK! This is the only thing that you can add to it because
                 // null belongs to any class.
```

We may call get() but we don't know the return type either:

```
List<?> list1;
Object obj = list1.get(0); //Can only declare it as Object
```

If there is another variable "list2" like below, can you assign list2 to list1?

```
List<?> list1;
List<String> list2;
list1 = list2; //OK?
```

To answer that question, you need to note the meaning of list2 having the type of List<String>. It means that list2 is asserting that the object it points to has an add() method that accepts an object of the String type and a get() method that returns an object of the String type:

```
class List<String> {
    void add(String obj);
    String get(int idx);
}
```

If we let list1 point to the object pointed to by list2, the assertion made by list1 is still true. In contrast, if we let list2 point to the object pointed to by list1, the assertion made by list2 is no longer true because the get() method of that object may not return a String, even though its add() method does accept a String (and others):

```
List<?> list1;
List<String> list2;
List<?> list3;
list1 = list2; //OK!
list2 = list1; //Compile error
list1 = list3; //OK!
```

Instead of a plain "?", we could write:

```
List<? extends Animal> list1;
```

It means the variable list1 is asserting that the object it points to has an add() method that accepts an object of a type unknown to list1 but is still known to list1 to be a subclass of Animal (including Animal itself), and it has a get() method that returns a object of a type unknown to list1 but is still known to list1 to be a subclass of Animal:

```
class List<SOME-SUBCLASS-OF-Animal> {
   void add(SOME-SUBCLASS-OF-Animal obj);
   SOME-SUBCLASS-OF-Animal get(int idx);
}
```

It means that:

```
List<? extends Animal> list1;
list1.add(new Animal()); //Compile error. It may only accept Dog.
list1.add(new Dog()); //Compile error. It may only accept Cat or Animal.
Animal a = list1.get(0); //OK! It must be an Animal.
```

Can we assign some other lists to list1?

```
List<? extends Animal> list1;
List<String> list2;
List<Animal> list3;
List<Dog> list4;
List<? extends Animal> list5;
list1 = list2; //Compile error
list1 = list3; //OK. Accepting Animal is accepting a subclass of Animal.
list1 = list4; //OK. Accepting Dog is accepting a subclass of Animal.
list1 = list5; //OK. Still accepting a subclass of Animal.
```

In this case, Animal is called the "upper bound" of the wildcard type ("?"), as in the inheritance hierarchy.

You may wonder what is wildcard type used for? Suppose that you'd like to write a method to print all the objects in a List. You may try:

```
class ListPrinter {
   static void print(List<Object> list) {
      //Call toString() on each element of the list & print the string
   }
}
```

However, this doesn't work. For example:

```
List<String> list = new ArrayList<String>();
list.add("a");
list.add("b");
ListPrinter.print(list); //Compile error
```

This is because the compiler considers List<String> completely unrelated to

List<Object>. To solve this problem, do it this way:

```
class ListPrinter {
  static void print(List<?> list) {
    for (Iterator<?> iter = list.iterator(); iter.hasNext(); ) {
      Object obj = iter.next();
      System.out.println(obj.toString());
    }
  }
}
...
List<String> list = new ArrayList<String>();
list.add("a");
list.add("b");
ListPrinter.print(list); //OK to assign List<String> to List<?>
```

What if you'd like to print a list of Animals only? You may try:

```
class AnimalPrinter {
  static void print(List<Animal> list) {
    ...
  }
}
```

But this won't work because it won't accept List<Dog> which is completely unrelated to List<Animal>. If you used List<?>, then it would accept List<String>. To solve this problem, do it this way:

```
class Animal {
  String getName() {
    ...
  }
}
class AnimalPrinter {
  static void print(List<? extends Animal> list) {
    for (Iterator<? extends Animal> iter = list.iterator();
       iter.hasNext(); ) {
      Animal a = iter.next();
      System.out.println(a.getName());
    }
  }
}
```

Note that "?" is not the same as a type parameter. It is used as a value (the actual type) for a type parameter. A type parameter is a type that will be specified. A wildcard type is a type that is unknown by the variable.

Constraining a type parameter

Confusingly, the upper bound can also be applied to a type parameter. For example, if the TreeSet requires its element to implement Comparable, it may be written as:

```
class TreeSet<E extends Comparable> implements Set<E> {
  ...
}
```

Then, in the raw type, E will be changed to Comparable instead of Object in the code of TreeSet. This will also allow you to write code like:

```
class TreeSet<E extends Comparable> implements Set<E> {
  ...
  void g() {
    E e1, e2;
    if (e1.compareTo(e2) < 0) {
```

```
      ...
    }
  }
}
```

When specifying the actual type, the compiler will check to make sure it implements Comparable:

```
TreeSet<Animal> t1; //Compile error
TreeSet<String> t2; //OK as String implements Comparable
```

Writing generic methods

Suppose that you'd like to write a method to return the maximum element in a List. You can do it this way:

```
public class MaxUtil {
  //<E> must appear right before the return type (happens to be E). It
  //is telling the compiler that this method has a type parameter.
  public static <E> E max(List<E> list) {
    ...
  }
}
```

Note that the class is not a generic class, but the method is a generic method. How to specify the actual type for E? The compiler will infer it from the arguments of the method call:

```
List<String> list1;
String s = MaxUtil.max(list1); //from list1, it knows E=String.
// So it will know the return value is a String. So it can check.
Integer i = MaxUtil.max(list1); //Compile error
```

Just like generic classes, the primary purpose of using generic methods is to perform compile-time checking of the arguments and the return values.

Actually, this method has a problem: It should make sure E implements Comparable. To fix it, you can constrain E when it is introduced:

```
public class MaxUtil {
  public static <E extends Comparable> E max(List<E> list) {
    ...
  }
}
```

Note that it is an error to write:

```
public class MaxUtil {
  public static <E> E max(List<E extends Comparable> list) {
    ...
  }
}
```

This is because you must constrain a type variable when it is introduced, not when it is used.

Specifying a lower bound

In fact, Comparable has been made a generic in JSE 5.0:

```
interface Comparable<T> {
  int compareTo(T obj);
}
```

Here you use T instead of E. It doesn't make any difference. E was used because the object was an element of a collection. Here T is used to mean any type.

Anyway, the max() method should use a parameterized type, not the raw type:

```
public class MaxUtil {
  public static <E extends Comparable<E>> E max(List<E> list) {
    ...
  }
}
```

This will work for cases like:

```
class Animal {
}
class Dog extends Animal implements Comparable<Dog> {
  int compareTo(Dog obj) {
    ...
  }
}
...
List<Dog> list1;
Dog d = MaxUtil.max(list1);
```

But what if the code is:

```
class Animal implements Comparable<Animal> {
  int compareTo(Animal obj) {
    ...
  }
}
class Dog extends Animal {
}
...
List<Dog> list1;
Dog d = MaxUtil.max(list1); //Compile error. E=Dog, but E doesn't
//implements Comparable<Dog>. It implements Comparable<Animal>.
```

The problem here is that E doesn't need to implement Comparable<E>. All it needs is to implement Comparable<?> in which "?" is a super class of E (including E itself). This can be written as:

```
public class MaxUtil {
  public static <E extends Comparable<? super E>> E max(List<E> list) {
    ...
  }
}
```

Here you are specifying E as the lower bound of the wildcard type, as in the inheritance hierarchy.

Use a wildcard or a type variable?

Consider the print() method again:

```
static void print(List<? extends Animal> list) {
  ...
}
```

Can you write it as:

```
static <E extends Animal> void print(List<E> list) {
  ...
}
```

Yes, you can. It will work just fine. The difference is that now it is a generic method but the original is just a regular method. So which one should you use? Note that in the generic version, E is used only once. In that case it's easier to use a wildcard. Only when it is used multiple times, should you use a type variable. For example, E is used twice in the code below:

```
public static <E> E max(List<E> list) {
   ...
}
```

Integrating legacy code with generic-aware code

You probably have code that uses the non-generic versions of List, Set and Map:

```
class Animal {
  boolean isTropical() {
    ...
  }
}
class Zoo {
  List inhabitants;

  void enter(List newComers) {
    for (int i = 0; i < newComers.size(); i++) {
      Animal a = (Animal)newComers.get(i);
      if (!a.isTropical()) {
        inhabitants.add(a);
      }
    }
  }
}
```

What does the raw type mean when it is compiled in JSE 5.0? Basically the compiler treats the direct use of the raw type List as List<?>, so the code would be like:

```
class Zoo {
  List<?> inhabitants;

  void enter(List<?> newComers) {
    for (int i = 0; i < newComers.size(); i++) {
      Animal a = (Animal)newComers.get(i);
      if (!a.isTropical()) {
        //If the type were really List<?> this wouldn't be allowed!
        inhabitants.add(a);
      }
    }
  }
}
```

Note that if the inhabitants variable were really declared as List<?>, then the call to add() would be rejected as a compile error because it is unknown whether it is a List of Animal or not. However, when the compiler is unsure (it may or may not work) and the type is a raw type, the compiler will figure that it is legacy code, give it the benefit of the doubt and allow it with a warning of "unchecked conversion".

To suppress the warning, you may:

```
class Zoo {
  List inhabitants;

  @SuppressWarnings("unchecked")
```

```
  void enter(List newComers) {
    for (int i = 0; i < newComers.size(); i++) {
      Animal a = (Animal)newComers.get(i);
      if (!a.isTropical()) {
        inhabitants.add(a);
      }
    }
  }
}
```

This is called an "annotation". It is telling the compiler to suppress the warnings about unchecked conversion in the following method.

So this code itself is OK. Can it be used by clients that are using generics?

```
List<Animal> newComers;
Zoo zoo;
zoo.enter(newComers); //OK?
```

Because the newComers is declared as the raw type and is basically treated as a List<?>, the call will be allowed and everything will work.

What if it is the reverse: The Zoo class is now using generics but the clients aren't?

```
class Zoo {
  List<Animal> inhabitants;

  void enter(List<Animal> newComers) {
    ...
  }
}
...
List newComers;
Zoo zoo;
zoo.enter(newComers); //OK?
```

If the newComers variable were declared as List<?>, then the call to enter() would be rejected as a compile error because it is unknown whether it is a List of Animal or not:

```
...
List<?> newComers;
Zoo zoo;
zoo.enter(newComers); //Error
```

However, it is declared as the raw type and the compiler is giving it the benefit of the doubt again: it will let it pass with a warning:

```
List newComers;
Zoo zoo;
zoo.enter(newComers); //Compile warning: unchecked conversion
```

To suppress the warning, can you type cast it?

```
List newComers;
Zoo zoo;
zoo.enter((List<Animal>)newComers); //Compile warning: unchecked conversion
```

You can type cast it but this is not a normal type cast. List<Animal> exists only at compile time, but type cast is done at runtime. So it doesn't really make sense. However, Java allows it with a warning. At runtime it will cast it to the raw type only (List), not to the parameterized type (List<Animal>). So all it does is to convince the compiler that it is a List<Animal> at compile-time.

To really suppress the warning, use the @SuppressWarnings annotation again. By the way, this can be done for a method or for a whole class:

```
@SuppressWarnings("unchecked")
class Foo {
  ...
  void g() {
    List newComers;
    Zoo zoo;
    zoo.enter(newComers);
  }
}
```

Of course, you're recommended to use it on a scope as small as possible (method) so that you don't suppress warnings that you aren't expecting.

Generics and method overriding

Check the code below:

```
class Foo {
  void g(List<String> list) {
    System.out.println("a");
  }
}
class Bar extends Foo {
  void g(List<String> list) {
    System.out.println("b");
  }
}
...
Foo f = new Bar();
f.g(new ArrayList<String>());
```

It will print "b". However, you may also override the g() method using the erasure of the method signature:

```
class Foo {
  void g(List<String> list) {
    System.out.println("a");
  }
}
class Bar extends Foo {
  void g(List list) {
    System.out.println("b");
  }
}
...
Foo f = new Bar();
f.g(new ArrayList<String>());
```

It will still work and print "b". Why allow it? The purpose is that a library developer (the person writing Foo) can use generic code while still allowing the library clients (Bar) to use non-generic code.

As another example, the Comparable interface is like:

```
class Comparable<T> {
  int compareTo(T obj);
}
```

To override it, you may write:

```
class Animal implements Comparable<Animal> {
  public int compareTo(Animal obj) {
    ...
  }
}
```

This gives a signature of:

```
int compareTo(Animal obj);
```

Or use the erasure of the signature:

```
class Animal implements Comparable {
  public int compareTo(Object obj) {
    ...
  }
}
```

The erasure of T is its upper bound (Object in this case).

This gives a signature of:

```
int compareTo(T obj);
```

Now, let's compare the code below:

Case 1	Case 2
```class Foo {` ` List<String> g() {` ` ...` ` }` `}` `class Bar extends Foo {` ` List g() {` ` ...` ` }` `}` `...` `Foo f = new Bar();` `List<String> list = f.g();```	```class Foo {` ` void g(List<String> list) {` ` ...` ` }` `}` `class Bar extends Foo {` ` void g(List<String> list) {` ` ...` ` }` `}` `...` `Foo f = new Bar();` `f.g(new ArrayList<String>());```

In case 2, the g() in Bar is accepting any List, while the g() in Foo is accepting only a List<String>. So it is accepting more arguments, but it will not break the promise of the g() in Foo. It is just more capable. In contrast, in case 1, the g() in Foo is saying that it will only return a List<String>, so its clients are only prepared to handle a List<String>. But the g() in Bar is saying that it will return any List. This may catch the clients by surprise because they are not prepared to handle any List, but just a List<String>. Therefore, the following line will trigger an unchecked warning:

```
class Foo {
  List<String> g() {
    ...
  }
}
class Bar extends Foo {
  List g() { //unchecked warning
    ...
  }
}
```

To suppress it, again, you can use a @SuppressWarnings:

```
class Foo {
  List<String> g() {
    ...
  }
}
```

```
class Bar extends Foo {
  @SuppressWarnings("unchecked")
  List g() {
    ...
  }
}
```

Generics and method name overloading

Check the code below:

```
class Foo {
  void g(List<String> list) {
    System.out.println("a");
  }
  void g(List<Integer> list) {
    System.out.println("b");
  }
}
```

It is trying to overload the method name "g". Will it work? No. If it were allowed, what would happen if there were a class Bar trying to override the g() method:

```
class Foo {
  void g(List<String> list) {
    System.out.println("a");
  }
  void g(List<Integer> list) {
    System.out.println("b");
  }                       It is the erasure of both, so which g() is
}                         it overriding?
class Bar extends Foo {
  void g(List list) {
    System.out.println("c");
  }
}
```

Therefore, it is forbidden to have two methods with the same name and whose parameter types have the same erasure.

Common mistakes

It is a mistake to use instanceof with a parameterized type:

```
List list1;
if (list1 instanceof List<String>) { //Compile error
  ...
}
```

It is a mistake to try to access the class object of a parameterized type:

```
Class c = List<String>.class; //Compile error
Object obj = List<String>.class.newInstance(); //Compile error
```

It is a mistake to use the type parameter in static members:

```
class List<E> {
  static E lastAccessed; //Compile error

  static boolean isValid(E obj) { //Compile error
    ...
```

```
    }
}
```

This is because static members are associated with the class, not with each object nor variable.

It is a mistake to use a primitive type as the value for a type variable:

```
List<int> list; //Compile error
```

This is because List<E> is compiled as if E were Object. Therefore, the actual type must a class, not a primitive type.

Summary

If there is a certain relationship between the type of the formal parameters and/or the return of a method at compile time, you should introduce type variables to express the relationship, making the method generic. If such a relationship spans across several methods in a class, you should make the whole class generic.

Type variables and parameterized types only exist at compile time, not at runtime. At runtime only their raw types exist. Therefore, you can't use instanceof on them, get their Class objects or create an array of them.

Different parameterized types of the same raw type are completely unrelated. They are assignment incompatible. The only exceptions are those using wildcards or raw types (legacy code).

If you'd like to write a method that deals with an unknown type, you can either use a type variable or a wildcard to represent the unknown type. If it is only used once, use a wildcard, otherwise use a type variable.

If the method is processing a parameterized type (e.g., a collection) and you're going to get objects of a certain type from it (e.g., get()), usually you will constrain the unknown type with an upper bound. If you're going to put objects of a certain type into it (e.g., add(XXX)) or just pass objects of a certain type to it (e.g., compareTo(XXX)), usually you will constrain the unknown type with a lower bound.

A raw type is basically considered the same as a parameterized type with its type variables bound to wildcards. However, to support legacy code, if you try to do something risky with a raw type (may or may not work), the compiler will allow it and issue an unchecked warning. For a parameterized type it will flag it as an error.

You can override a method using the same signature or the erasure of the signature. If the erasure occurs for a parameter, it is fine. If it occurs for the return type, it will trigger an unchecked warning. Because you can override a method using its erasure, you can't have two methods of the same name that have the same erasure.

Review questions

6. How to create a Set that will contain some Foo objects?

```
_____ s = new _____ ();
```

7. Given the code below:

```
class Foo {
}
class Bar extends Foo {
}
...
List<Foo> l1;
List<Bar> l2;
List<?> l3;
List<? extends Foo> l4;
List<? super Foo> l5;
List l6;
List<Object> l7;
```

Can each of the following compile? If yes, will there be any warning?

Statement	Compile? (Yes/No/Warning)
l1=l2;	
l2=l1;	
l1=l3;	
l3=l1;	
l1=l4;	
l4=l1;	
l4=l2;	
l1=l5;	
l5=l1;	
l5=l7;	
l1=l6;	
l6=l1;	
l3=l7;	
l7=l3;	
l3=l6;	
l6=l3;	

8. Will the code below compile?

```
List<String> l1 = new ArrayList<String>();
List l2 = l1;
if (l2 instanceof List<String>) {
```

```
  . . .
}
```

9. Will the code below compile?

```
Object[] a = new ArrayList<String>[10];
```

10. Write a generic interface to represent a stack of objects of some type T. It should have a push() method to put an object onto the top and a pop() method that removes the top object and returns it.

11. How to suppress an unchecked warning?

12. Will the code below compile? If yes, any warning?

```
Set<String> l1 = new HashSet<String>();
Set<?> l2 = l1;
l2.add("a");
```

13. Will the code below compile? If yes, any warning?

```
Set<String> l1 = new HashSet<String>();
Set l2 = l1;
l2.add("a");
```

14. Write the signature for a method that can add an object to a generic Set. For example, it can add an Integer to a Set<Integer>.

15. Improve the signature above so that if Bar is a subclass of Foo, you can add a Bar object to a Set<Bar> or Set<Foo>.

16. Write the signature for a method that takes a File object and a List of objects that implement Serializable. The method will write them into the file.

17. Assuming Bar is a subclass of Foo. Write the signature for a method that takes a List of Foo objects and a keyword (a string). Then the method will return the first Foo object whose string representation contains that keyword. Make sure it accepts a List of Bar objects.

18. Will the code below compile?

```
class Foo<T1, T2> {
  void g(T1 a) {
  }
  void g(T2 a) {
  }
}
```

19. Will the code below compile?

```
class Foo<T1, T2 extends Foo> {
  void g(T1 a) {
  }
  void g(T2 a) {
  }
}
```

Answers to review questions

1. How to create a Set that will contain some Foo objects?

```
Set<Foo> s = new HashSet<Foo>();
```

2. Given the code below:

```
class Foo {
}
class Bar extends Foo {
}
...
List<Foo> l1;
List<Bar> l2;
List<?> l3;
List<? extends Foo> l4;
List<? super Foo> l5;
List l6;
List<Object> l7;
```

Can each of the following compile? If yes, will there be any warning?

Statement	Compile? (Yes/No/Warning)	Explanation
l1=l2;	N	Different parameterized types are completely unrelated.
l2=l1;	N	Ditto
l1=l3;	N	l3 is a List of unknown. It may be List<Foo> or List<String>. So the compiler is unsure and will prohibit it.
l3=l1;	Y	A List<Foo> is certainly a List of something. This won't break the assertion made by l3.
l1=l4;	N	l4 could be List<Foo> or List<Bar>. So it is not always valid to assign it to l1.
l4=l1;	Y	A List<Foo> is certainly a List of some type that extends Foo.
l4=l2;	Y	A List<Bar> is certainly a List of some type that extends Foo.
l1=l5;	N	l5 could be List<Foo> or List<Object> (Object is a base class of Foo). So it is not always valid to assign it to l1.
l5=l1;	Y	A List<Foo> is certainly a List of some type that is a base class of Foo.

Statement	Compile? (Yes/No/Warning)	Explanation
I5=I7;	Y	Object is a base class of Foo.
I1=I6;	W	I6 could be List<Foo> or List<String>. The compiler is unsure but as it is using the raw type, it is legacy code so it is allowed with a warning.
I6=I1;	Y	I6 is just like List<?>, so it can always accept a List<Foo>.
I3=I7;	Y	Any List is a List<?>, including List<Object>.
I7=I3;	N	List<Object> is just like List<Foo> or List<Bar>. It can only accept a List<Object>, not even List<Foo> or anything else.
I3=I6;	Y	List and List<?> are basically the same thing.
I6=I3;	Y	List and List<?> are basically the same thing.

3. Will the code below compile?

```
List<String> l1 = new ArrayList<String>();
List l2 = l1;
if (l2 instanceof List<String>) {
  ...
}
```

No, a parameterized type doesn't exist at runtime and thus can't be checked with instanceof.

4. Will the code below compile?

```
Object[] a = new ArrayList<String>[10];
```

No, a parameterized type doesn't exist at runtime and thus can't be used as the element type of an array.

5. Write a generic interface to represent a stack of objects of some type T. It should have a push() method to put an object onto the top and a pop() method that removes the top object and returns it.

```
interface Stack<T> {
  void push(T obj);
  T pop();
}
```

6. How to suppress an unchecked warning?

@SuppressWarnings("unchecked")

7. Will the code below compile? If yes, any warning?

```
Set<String> l1 = new HashSet<String>();
Set<?> l2 = l1;
l2.add("a");
```

No, you can't call add() because the element type is unknown. It could be a String or an Integer. As the compiler is unsure, it won't allow it.

8. Will the code below compile? If yes, any warning?

```
Set<String> l1 = new HashSet<String>();
Set l2 = l1;
l2.add("a");
```

Yes. The case is similar to the previous question. However, this is still allowed (with an unchecked warning) because the code is using Set and is therefore considered legacy code.

9. Write the signature for a method that can add an object to a generic Set. For example, it can add an Integer to a Set<Integer>.

```
static <E> void add(Set<E> s, E element);
```

10. Improve the signature above so that if Bar is a subclass of Foo, you can add a Bar object to a Set<Bar> or Set<Foo>.

```
static <E> void add(Set<? super E> s, E element);
```

11. Write the signature for a method that takes a File object and a List of objects that implement Serializable. The method will write them into the file.

```
static void writeToFile(File f, List<? extends Serializable> list);
```

You could write a generic method:

```
static <T extends Serializable> void writeToFile(File f, List<T> list);
```

But this is not as good because T is only used once.

12. Assuming Bar is a subclass of Foo. Write the signature for a method that takes a List of Foo objects and a keyword (a string). Then the method will return the first Foo object whose string representation contains that keyword. Make sure it accepts a List of Bar objects.

You may try:

```
static Foo search(List<? extends Foo> list, String keyword);
```

However, it will return a Foo object even if the list is List<Bar>. Ideally, it should return a Bar object in that case.

A better way is to make sure the return type is the same as the element type of the List:

```
static <T extends Foo> T search(List<T> list, String keyword);
```

13. Will the code below compile?

```
class Foo<T1, T2> {
  void g(T1 a) {
  }
  void g(T2 a) {
  }
}
```

No. The signatures of the two methods have the same non-generic version:

```
void g(Object a);
void g(Object a);
```

14. Will the code below compile?

```
class Foo<T1, T2 extends Foo> {
  void g(T1 a) {
  }
  void g(T2 a) {
  }
}
```

Yes. The non-generic versions of their signatures are different:

```
void g(Object a);
void g(Foo a);
```

Mock exam

5. How to create a Map that maps a student # (a string) to a Student object?

    a. new HashMap();

    b. new HashMap<String, Student>();

    c. new HashMap<String><Student>();

    d. new HashMap[String, Student]();

6. What is true about the following code?

```
14. public abstract class Shape {
15.    public abstract void draw();
16. }
17. public class Rect extends Shape {
18.    ...
19.    public Rect(int w, int h) {
20.       ...
21.    }
22.    public void draw() {
23.       ...
24.    }
25. }
26. ...
27. Set<Rect> s = new HashSet<Rect>();
28. s.add(new Rect(5, 3));
29. for (Iterator<Rect> iter = s.iterator(); iter.hasNext(); ) {
30.    Rect r = (Rect)iter.next();
31.    ...
32. }
```

    a. There will be a warning at line 14.

    b. There will be a compilation error at line 15.

    c. There will be a compilation error at line 16.

    d. There is no need to typecast at line 17.

7. Assuming the same Shape and Rect classes as above, what is true about the following code?

```
1.  Set<Shape> s = new HashSet<Shape>();
2.  s.add(new Rect(5, 3));
```

    a. There will be a compilation error at line 1.

    b. There will be a compilation error at line 2.

    c. There will be a runtime error at line 2.

    d. It will compile and run just fine.

8. Assuming the same Shape and Rect classes as above, what is true about the following code?

```
1.  Set<Shape> s = new HashSet<Rect>();
2.  s.add(new Rect(5, 3));
```

    a. There will be a compilation error at line 1.

b. There will be a runtime error at line 1.

c. There will be a compilation error at line 2.

d. There will be a runtime error at line 2.

e. It will compile and run just fine.

9. Assuming the same Shape and Rect classes as above, what is true about the following code?

```
1.   Set<Rect> s = new HashSet<Rect>();
2.   Shape sh = new Rect(5, 3);
3.   s.add(sh);
```

a. There will be a compilation error at line 1.

b. There will be a compilation error at line 2.

c. There will be a compilation error at line 3.

d. It will compile and run just fine.

10. Assuming the same Shape and Rect classes as above, in order to write a method that draws all the Shapes (could also be Rect objects) in a Collection, what should you fill in the blank?

```
1.   void drawAll(Collection<_____> c) {
2.      ...
3.   }
```

a. Shape

b. Object

c. ? extends Shape

d. ? super Rect

e. ?

11. Assuming the same Shape and Rect classes as above, what is true about the following code?

```
1.   Collection<String> c1 = new ArrayList<String>();
2.   Collection<?> c2 = c1;
3.   Collection<String> c3 = c2;
```

a. There will be a compilation error at line 1.

b. There will be a compilation error at line 2.

c. There will be a compilation error at line 3.

d. It will compile and run just fine.

12. Assuming the same Shape and Rect classes as above, what is true about the following code?

```
1.   Collection<String> c1 = new ArrayList<String>();
2.   Collection c2 = c1;
3.   Collection<String> c3 = c2;
```

a. There will be a compilation error at line 1.

b. There will be a compilation error at line 2.

c. There will be a warning at line 2.

d. There will be a compilation error at line 3.

e. There will be a warning at line 3.

f. It will compile and run just fine.

13. Assuming the same Shape and Rect classes as above, if you'd like to write a static method to move all the Shapes (could be Rect objects) in one collection c1 to another collection c2, what should the signature be? It should support all move operations that make sense (e.g., moving elements from a List of Rect into a Set of Object or a List of Shape or a List of Rect).

a. static void move(Collection<Shape> c1, Collection<Shape> c2)

b. static void move(Collection<? super Shape> c1, Collection<? extends Shape> c2)

c. static void move(Collection<? extends Shape> c1, Collection<? super Shape> c2)

d. static <T extends Shape> void move(Collection<T> c1, Collection<? super T> c2)

14. What is true about the following code?

```
1.  HashSet<String> s1 = new HashSet<String>();
2.  HashSet s2 = s1;
3.  if (s2 instanceof HashSet<Integer>) {
4.     System.out.println("Y");
5.  } else {
6.     System.out.println("N");
7.  }
```

a. It will print "Y".

b. It will print "N".

c. It will throw a ClassCastException at line 3.

d. It will not compile.

Answers to the mock exam

1. b.

2. d. The iterator is a Iterator<Rect>, so its next() method will return a Rect.

3. d. The add() method accepts a Shape. As a Rect is a Shape, it is also accepted.

4. a. A variable of type HashSet<Rect> points to an object that has an add() method accepting a Rect only (but not other Shapes). A variable of type Set<Shape> points to an object that has an add() method accepting any Shape. If you assign the first object to the second variable, the assertion of the second variable may no longer be true.

5. c. Even though the "sh" variable points to a Rect object at runtime, the compiler doesn't know that. It only looks at the type of the "sh" variable (at compile time) which is Shape. As the add() method accepts a Rect only, it is unsure whether that object can be passed to the add() method. So it treats it as an error.

6. c.

   a. Collection<Shape> will not accept Collection<Rect>.

   b. Collection<Object> will only accept Collection<Object> and nothing else.

   c. Collection<? extends Shape> is the correct answer.

   d. Collection<? super Rect> will accept Collection<Shape> and Collection<Rect>, but it will also accept Collection<Object>, so it is too broad.

   e. Similarly, Collection<?> will accept too much.

7. c. The compiler is unsure whether this List<?> is a List<String>. It only looks at the type of the variable (at compile time), not the object it points to at runtime.

8. e. The case is similar to the previous question, but this time the raw type is used. The compiler is still unsure, but it will allow it with a warning.

9. d.

   a. static void move(Collection<Shape> c1, Collection<Shape> c2). c1 will only accept Collection<Shape>, not Collection<Rect>.

   b. static void move(Collection<? super Shape> c1, Collection<? extends Shape> c2). c1 will not accept Collection<Rect>.

   c. static void move(Collection<? extends Shape> c1, Collection<? super Shape> c2). c1 will accept Collection<Shape> or Collection<Rect>. c2 will accept Collection<Shape> or Collection<Object>. However, c2 won't accept Collection<Rect> even if c1 is Collection<Rect>.

d. static <T extends Shape> void move(Collection<T> c1, Collection<? super T> c2). This is the correct answer. c1 will accept Collection<Shape> or Collection<Rect>. If it is a Collection<Rect>, then c2 will accept Collection<Object>, Collection<Shape> or Collection<Rect>.

10.d. You can't use a parameterized type with the instanceof operator because it doesn't exist at runtime.

Chapter 3

For-each loop

What's in this chapter?

In this chapter you'll learn how to use the for-each loop.

For-each loop

To iterate over say a List of Foo objects, you'd write something like:

```
List<Foo> fs;
for (Iterator<Foo> iter = fs.iterator(); iter.hasNext(); ) {
  Foo f = iter.next();
  ...
}
```

In JSE 5.0, there is a simpler way:

```
List<Foo> fs;
for (Foo f: fs) { //it reads: for each Foo object f in fs
  ...
}
```

This is called a "For-each" loop. It will loop through each Foo object in fs and assign each one to the f variable in turn. That is, it does exactly the same thing as the original code. But how does it work?

When the compiler sees a for-each loop (see the diagram below), it will try to generate an old style loop using an Iterator. It doesn't know it is an Iterator of what type yet. It will copy the expression after the colon ("fs") and then call the iterator() method on it to get an Iterator. But how can it be sure that it has an iterator() method? It will check if this expression implements the Iterable<T> interface. In this case, it notes that the List<T> interface extends the Collection<T> and the Collection<T> interface in turn extends Iterable<T>, so List<T> inherits the iterator() method from Iterable<T>. Therefore, List<Foo> does have an iterator() method that returns an Iterator<Foo>. Now, it knows it should use an Iterator<Foo> in the loop. Then, it copies the declaration of the loop variable ("Foo f") into the loop body and use it to store the return value of iter.next():

9: Therefore, List<Foo> will inherit such
an Iterator() method:

```
interface List<Foo> {
    Iterator<Foo> iterator();
}
```

```
interface Iterable<T> {
    Iterator<T> iterator();
}
```

10: Now I know it returns an Iterator of Foo.

8: I know Collection<T>
implements Iterable<T>

1: Look, we have a for-each loop here.

6: Does it implement Iterable? I know
List<T> implements Collection<T>
which implements Iterable<T>.

```
interface Collection<T> {
    ...
}
```

7: I know List<T>
implements
Collection<T>

5: Does it implement
Iterable? Need to
check its declaration:

```
interface List<T> {
    ...
}
```

```
List<Foo> fs;
for (Foo f: fs) {
    ...
}
```

3: Copy whatever
expression into
into here.

2: Generate a for loop using an
Iterator. But I don't know it is an
Iterator of what type yet:

4: Call iterator() on it. But how to make
sure it has such a method? So, check if fs
implements the Iterable interface which is:

12: Copy

```
for (Iterator<???> iter = fs.iterator(); iter.hasNext(); ) {
    Foo f = iter.next();
    ...
}
```

11: Fill in "Foo" here

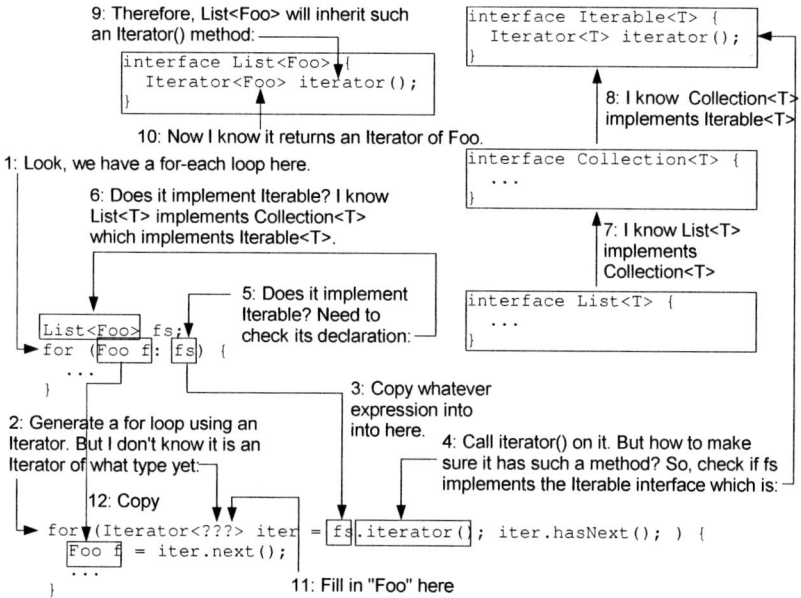

Note that the type of the loop variable doesn't have to be the same as the
element type of the Iterable. For example:

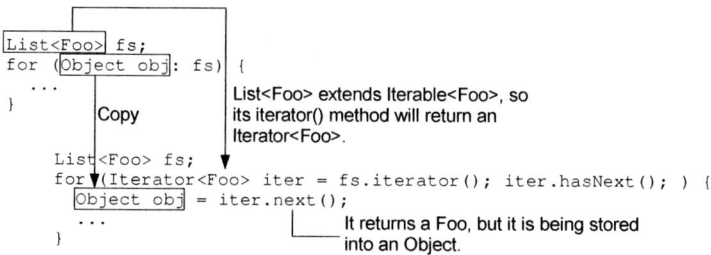

```
List<Foo> fs;
for (Object obj: fs) {
    ...
}
```

Copy

List<Foo> extends Iterable<Foo>, so
its iterator() method will return an
Iterator<Foo>.

```
List<Foo> fs;
for (Iterator<Foo> iter = fs.iterator(); iter.hasNext(); ) {
    Object obj = iter.next();
    ...
}
```

It returns a Foo, but it is being stored
into an Object.

Because a Foo object is assignment compatible with Object, so it will work
fine. In contrast, the following won't work:

```
List<Object> fs;
for (Foo f: fs) {
    ...
}
```

Because the translated code would be:

```
List<Object> fs;
for (Iterator<Object> iter = fs.iterator(); iter.hasNext(); ) {
    Foo f = iter.next(); //iter.next() returns an Object, can't assign to Foo
    ...
}
```

Because the java.util.Collection<T> interface extends Iterable<T>, you can
use a for-each loop on its implementations like a List or a Set (but not a Map
because the Map interface does NOT extend the Collection interface).

The for-each loop works with arrays too:

```
int[] a = {2, 4, 1};
for (int i: a) {
  ...
}
```

The compiler will translate the code into a loop using an index variable (just like an iterator):

```
int[] a = {2, 4, 1};
for (int idx = 0; idx < a.length; idx++) {
  int i = a[idx];
  ...
}
```

Because you can't have a List of primitives such as List<int>, you may use a List<Integer> instead. In that case, to iterate on it, the loop variable may be an Integer, but it can also be an int because an Integer is assignment compatible with an int thanks to auto unboxing:

```
List<Integer> list = ...;
for (Integer i: list) { //OK
  ...
}
for (int i: list) { //OK. Integer is assignment compatible with int
  ...
}
```

Summary

A for-each loop allows you to iterate through an object that implements the Iterable interface. It also works on an array.

Review questions

15. The for-each loop works with an object that implements _____ or an _____.

16. The code below is trying to print out a collection of Integers. Fill out the blanks:

```
Collection<Integer> c = ...;
for (_____) {
  System.out.println(_____);
}
```

Answers to review questions

1. The for-each loop works with an object that implements <u>Iterable</u> or an <u>array</u>.

2. The code below is trying to print out a collection of Integers. Fill out the blanks:

```
Collection<Integer> c = ...;
for (Integer i: c) {
  System.out.println(i);
}
```

If you'd like, you could use auto unboxing:

```
Collection<Integer> c = ...;
for (int i: c) {
  System.out.println(i);
}
```

Mock exam

11. To loop through a collection of Foo objects, what should you fill in the blank?

```
1.  Collection<Foo> fs = ...;
2.  for (_____) {
3.     ...
4.  }
```

a. Foo foo in fs

b. Foo foo: fs

c. foo in fs

d. foo: fs

12. In order to use a for-each loop on an object (which is not an array), what must be true?

a. It must implement the Iterable interface.

b. It must implement the Iterator interface.

c. It must implement the Collection interface.

d. It must extend the Loopable class.

Answers to the mock exam

1. b.
2. a.

Chapter 4

Manipulating Collections

What's in this chapter?

In this chapter you'll learn how to sort and search collections and arrays and etc.

Sorting and searching a List

Suppose you have a List of strings and would like to sort it, you can use the java.util.Collections class (note the "s" at the end. It's not the same as the java.util.Collection interface):

```
List<String> list;
Collections.sort(list);
```

This static method will sort the list in ascending order (thus the list is modified). It assumes that the class of the element already implements Comparable and will call compareTo() on the elements to determine their ordering. This is indeed the case for the String class. If not, you need to specify a Comparator:

```
List<Foo> list;
Comparator<Foo> c;
Collections.sort(list, c);
```

If a list is sorted, you can also search for a certain element in the list using binary search:

```
List<String> list;
Collections.sort(list);
int idx = Collections.binarySearch(list, "f");
if (idx >= 0) { //found
    ...
}
```

Again, it is using the compareTo() method to look for the element. If found, the index of that element will be returned. If the class doesn't implement Comparable, you need to specify a Comparator:

```
List<Foo> list;
Comparator<Foo> c;
Collections.sort(list, c);
Collections.binarySearch(list, new Foo(), c);
```

What if the element is not found? The index is still useful: it indicates where you should insert that element to keep the list sorted. For example, if the list is "b", "e", "k" and you're searching for "f", the correct index to insert "f" should be 2. If it returned 2 to you, you couldn't tell whether the element was found at index 2 or was not found but should be inserted at index 2. So it returns -2 to you.

However, there is still a minor problem. If you are searching for "a", the correct index to insert "a" should be 0. If it returns -0, then it is just 0. Then you can't tell whether it is found at index 0 or not found and should be inserted at index 0. So, after negating the index (2=>-2, 0=>-0), it will always minus 1 from it (2=>-3, 0=>-1) so that the return values for all not-found cases will be strictly negative.

To make use of this return value, do something like this:

```
...
int idx = Collections.binarySearch(list, "f");
if (idx >= 0) { //found
    ...
} else { //not found
    int insertIdx = -(idx+1); //add 1 to undo the -1. Then negate it.
    list.add(insertIdx, "f");
}
```

Note that even though the sort() method and the binarySearch() method are in the Collections class, they only work on a List, but not on a Set because a Set has no concept of ordering.

Sorting and searching an array

To sort an array, it is very similar to sorting a List. The difference is that you use the java.util.Arrays class instead of the java.util.Collections class:

```
String[] a1;
Arrays.sort(a1); //the class of the element implements Comparable
Foo[] a2;
Comparator<Foo> c;
Arrays.sort(a2, c); //specify a Comparator
```

It works for primitive values too:

```
int[] a1;
Arrays.sort(a1);
```

After sorting an array, you can use binary search to look for an element:

```
String[] a1;
Arrays.sort(a1);
int idx = Arrays.binarySearch(a1, "f");
Foo[] a2;
Comparator<Foo> c;
Arrays.sort(a2, c);
int idx = Arrays.binarySearch(a2, new Foo(), c);
```

The meaning of the return value is the same as that of Collections.binarySearch().

Converting a Collection into an array

To convert a Collection (List, Set) into an array:

```
List<String> list;
Object[] a1 = list.toArray();
```

It returns an Object array, each of whose elements is a String. Can you use it like this?

```
List<String> list;
Object[] a1 = list.toArray();
String[] a2 = (String[])a1; //OK?
```

No, you can't. In Java, when you create an array in Java, you must specify its element type:

```
Foo[] x = new Foo[10]; //element type is Foo
String[] y = new String[10]; //element type is String
```

```
Object[] z = new Object[10]; //element type is Object
```

Once the array is created, it stores that element type in itself and can't change that. So, a1 points to an array of Object and a2 can't point to that array.

Why does toArray() not create an array of String in the first place? Because unlike an array, a List object does NOT know its element type at runtime (generic only works at compile-time). To solve this problem, you may provide an array to it:

```
List<String> list;
String[] a2 = list.toArray(new String[100]);
```

Then it doesn't need to create the array and will simply store the elements into there. It will return a String[], so no typecasting is required. How it knows that it should return a String[] instead of say an Integer[]? The signature of the method is:

```
interface List<E> {
  <T> T[] toArray(T[] a);
}
```

It means that if you pass it an Integer[], it will return an Integer[]. You may wonder why it shouldn't be:

```
interface List<E> {
  E[] toArray(E[] a);
}
```

For a List<Animal>, it won't accept say Object[]. How about:

```
interface List<E> {
  <T super E> T[] toArray(T[] a);
}
```

For a List<Animal>, it won't accept say Dog[], but this should be allowed because the List<Animal> may contain Dogs only by incident. As the Dog[] will perform the checking at runtime to make sure the objects being added are indeed Dogs, there is no need to say "T super E".

Anyway, let's go back to check the code again:

```
List<String> list;
String[] a2 = list.toArray(new String[100]);
```

Hard-coding the size as 100 is not very good. A better way is:

```
List<String> list;
String[] a2 = list.toArray(new String[list.size()]);
```

Another way is to specify an empty array:

```
List<String> list;
String[] a2 = list.toArray(new String[0]);
```

If the array is not large enough, toArray() will clone it (to copy its element type) and use a correct size.

Converting an array into a List

To convert an array a1 to a List, you can't call a1.toList() because an array has no member methods. This function is provided by the Arrays class:

```
String[] a1;
List<String> list = Arrays.asList(a1);
```

Note that the returned List is just a wrapper over the array. That is, if you read an element in the List, the array element will be read. If you set an element in the List, the array element will be set. That is why the method is called asList() instead of toList(). In addition, the List is also fixed in size because no array can change its size. If you try to add or remove elements, it will throw an exception. To work around this limitation, you can make a copy of it:

```
String[] a1;
List<String> list = new ArrayList<String>(Arrays.asList(a1));
```

You can also pass individual elements instead of an array to make a List:

```
List<String> list = Arrays.asList("a", "d", "f");
```

This is very useful when you want to create a List with some fixed elements. In the past, you would have to add them one by one:

```
List<String> list = new ArrayList<String>();
list.add("a");
list.add("d");
list.add("f");
```

Note that while you can convert a Set to an array, but you can't convert an array back to a Set.

Summary

You can use the Collections class or the Arrays class to sort a List or an array. Make sure the elements implement Comparable, otherwise you need to provide a Comparator.

You can use the Collections class or the Arrays class to search for an element in a sorted List or array. If the element is found, the index is returned. If not found, the appropriate index to insert it is negated, subtracted by 1 and returned.

You can convert a Collection to an array by calling toArray() on the collection. You can convert an array to a List by calling Arrays.asList(). When converting a Collection to an array, usually it is incorrect to call the no-argument version of toArray() because it will create an Object[]. Instead, you probably should provide an array of the right element type to it. When converting an array to a List, the List is just a wrapper around the array and is therefore fixed in size.

Review questions

3. The code below is trying to sort a List of Integers. Fill out the blanks:

```
import java.util.List;
import _____;
...
List<Integer> list = ...;
_____._____(list);
```

4. If the List above is {18, 5, 25, 2}, after being sorted, it will become _____.

5. Can you use the method above to sort a Set or a Map?

6. The code below is trying to sort an array of Integers. Fill out the blanks:

```
import _____;
...
Integer[] a;
_____._____(a);
```

7. In order to sort a List or an array of some Foo objects that don't implement Comparable, what do you need to do?

8. To perform binary search on a List or an array, what condition must be met first?

9. If an array is {2, 5, 13, 26} and you perform a binary search on it for the value of 18, what is the return value?

10. Fill out the blanks:

```
List<Integer> list = new ArrayList<Integer>();
list.add(20);
list.add(40);
Integer[] a = list._____(_____);
```

11. Generally one can convert a _____ to an array using the method above.

12. Fill out the blanks:

```
Integer[] a = {3, 8, 4, 1};
List<Integer> list = _____._____(a);
```

13. What is the major limitation of a List converted from an array?

14. Generally one can convert an array to a _____ using the method above.

Answers to review questions

1. The code below is trying to sort a List of Integers. Fill out the blanks:

```
import java.util.List;
import java.util.Collections;
...
List<Integer> list = ...;
Collections.sort(list);
```

2. If the List above is {18, 5, 25, 2}, after being sorted, it will become {2, 5, 18, 25}.

3. Can you use the method above to sort a Set or a Map?

No, they have no concept of ordering.

4. The code below is trying to sort an array of Integers. Fill out the blanks:

```
import java.util.Arrays;
...
Integer[] a;
Arrays.sort(a);
```

5. In order to sort a List or an array of some Foo objects which don't implement Comparable, what do you need to do?

Provide a Comparator.

6. To perform binary search on a List or an array, what condition must be met first?

It has been sorted.

7. If an array is {2, 5, 13, 26} and you perform a binary search on it for the value of 18, what is the return value?

-4. It is not found and should be inserted at index 3. So it will return -3-1 which is -4.

8. Fill out the blanks:

```
List<Integer> list = new ArrayList<Integer>();
list.add(20);
list.add(40);
Integer[] a = list.toArray(new Integer[0]);
```

9. Generally one can convert a Collection to an array using the method above.

10. Fill out the blanks:

```
Integer[] a = {3, 8, 4, 1};
List<Integer> list = Arrays.asList(a);
```

11. What is the major limitation of a List converted from an array?

It can't change its size.

12. Generally one can convert an array to a List using the method above.

Mock exam

3. In order to sort a List<Integer> x, what should you do?

   a. Call x.sort().

   b. Call Collection.sort(x).

   c. Call Collections.sort(x).

   d. Call List.sort(x).

4. Fill in the code to test if an object is found in a sorted List:

```
5.    int idx = Collections.binarySearch(...);
6.    if (_____) {
7.       ...
8.    }
```

   a. idx >= 0

   b. idx > 0

   c. idx < 0

   d. !Integer.isNaN(idx)

5. What is true about the code below?

```
1.   class Foo {
2.      Integer[] g(List<Integer> list) {
3.         return (Integer[])list.toArray();
4.      }
5.   }
```

   a. There is a compile error at line 2.

   b. There is a compile error at line 3.

   c. There will be a runtime error at line 3.

   d. It will compile and run just fine.

6. What is true about the code below?

```
1.   Integer[] a = ...;
2.   List<Integer> list = Arrays.asList(a);
3.   list.add(10);
```

   a. There is a compile error at line 2.

   b. There is a compile error at line 3.

   c. There will be a runtime error at line 3.

   d. It will compile and run just fine.

Answers to the mock exam

1. c.

2. a. If it is found, it is the index and thus must be >= 0. If it is not found, the return value is strictly negative.

3. c. toArray() will return an Object[] which is not an Integer[].

4. c. The List converted from an array is fixed in size.

Chapter 5

Variable Arity Parameters

What's in this chapter?

In this chapter you'll learn how to allow a method to take a variable-number of arguments.

Using a vararg

You can see that you can pass as many as arguments to the Arrays.asList() method. How to write such a method? For example, you can write a method to add all the int values passed to it:

```
                                    ┌─── The compiler will treat it exactly the same as:
class Adder {
    static int add(int... ints) {                            ┌─────────┐
        int sum = 0;                                         │ int[]   │
        for (int i: ints) {                                   └─────────┘
            sum += i;                   They will be packed
        }                               into an array
        return sum;
    }      It is called a "variable arity parameter" or
}          "vararg". After seeing it, the compiler will
           mark the method as "accepting variable
           number of arguments". That is, it will allow
           calls like: ───────────────────── Adder.add(3, 6, 9, 1);
```

Before packing the arguments into an array, the compiler will first check if the argument is already an int[] (or something that can be assigned to an int[] such as null), if so, it won't perform the packing:

```
int[] a = new int[]{4, 3, 6};
int s1 = Adder.add(a); //already an int[], no packing required
int s2 = Adder.add(null); //can be assigned to an int[], no packing required
```

Note that the caller may provide 0 argument to it:

```
int s1 = Adder.add(); //OK
int s2 = Adder.add(new int[0]); //OK
```

So your add() method must be prepared for that.

Your method may have other "normal" parameters before the vararg, that is, it can have at most one vararg and it can only be the last parameter:

```
void g1(String s, int... ints) { //OK
}
void g2(int... ints, String s) { //Compile error
}
void g3(String s, int... ints, String... strings) { //Compile error
}
```

Vararg and method name overloading

Will the code below compile?

```
class Foo {
  void g(Foo[] a) {
  }
  void g(Foo... a) {
```

```
    }
}
```

No, it won't. As the vararg is treated exactly the same as an array, the two methods above have exactly the same argument types. Therefore, the attempt to overload will fail.

Check the code below:

```
class Foo {
  void g(String s1, String s2) {
  }
  void g(String... a) {
  }
}
...
Foo f = new Foo();
f.g("a", "b");
```

Which g() will it call? Just like autoboxing, when looking for an applicable method, at the beginning, methods using varargs are not considered. So only the first g() is found to be applicable and thus it will be used. If no applicable method is found, methods using varargs will be considered. For example, if the code were:

```
class Foo {
  void g(String s1, String s2) {
  }
  void g(String... a) {
  }
}
...
Foo f = new Foo();
f.g("a", "b", "c");
```

Then the first g() would be inapplicable. Then methods using varargs would be considered and the second g() would be used.

In fact, before trying the methods with varargs, autoboxing will be considered first. For example:

```
class Foo {
  void g(String s1, String s2) {
  }
  void g(String s, int i) {
  }
  void g(Object... a) {
  }
}
...
Foo f = new Foo();
f.g("a", "b");
f.g("a", 10);
f.g("a", new Integer(10));
f.g("a", new Double(10));
```

Without considering autoboxing and varargs, the first g() is found to be applicable and is used.

Without considering autoboxing and varargs, the second g() is found to be applicable and used.

Without considering autoboxing and varargs, no method is found to be applicable. Considering autoboxing, the second g() is found to be applicable and used.

Without considering autoboxing and varargs, no method is found to be applicable. Considering autoboxing, no method is found to be applicable. Considering varargs, the third g() is found to be applicable and used.

Vararg and method overriding

Check the code below:

```
class Foo {
```

```
  void g(Foo[] a) {
    System.out.println("a");
  }
}
class Bar extends Foo {
  void g(Foo... a) {
    System.out.println("b");
  }
}
...
Foo f = new Bar();
f.g(new Foo[]{ });
```

What will it do? It will print "b". However, this practice of overriding a method
not using a vararg with one using a vararg or vice versa is discouraged, so the
compiler will issue a warning.

Summary

A vararg is treated exactly as an array, with the added effect that the compiler
will pack the actual arguments into an array if required. A method can have at
most one vararg which (if any) must be the last parameter.

When looking for an applicable method, autoboxing and varargs are not
considered at first. If not found, then autoboxing is considered. If still not
found, varargs are considered.

Review questions

13. It is known that the signature of the main() method can be written using a vararg. Write the signature here.

14. What is the major limitation of a vararg?

Answers to review questions

1. It is known that the signature of the main() method can be written using a vararg. Write the signature here.

```
public static void main(String... args)
```

2. What is the major limitation of a vararg?

It must be the last parameter.

Mock exam

5. What is true about the code below?

```
1.  class Foo {
2.    static void g(String... args) {
3.      System.out.println(args.length);
4.    }
5.    static public void main(String[] args) {
6.      g("a", "b", "c");
7.      g(new String[]{"d", "e"});
8.      g();
9.    }
10. }
```

a. It will print 3, 2 and 0.

b. It will print 3, 1 and 0.

c. There is a compile error at line 2.

d. There is a compile error at line 3.

e. There is a compile error at line 6.

f. There is a compile error at line 7.

g. There is a compile error at line 8.

Answers to the mock exam

1. a. For the first call to g(), an array of three strings will be created. For the second call, the array is passed as is. For the third call, a new empty array will be created.

Chapter 6

Enum

What's in this chapter?

In this chapter you'll learn how to use enums.

Creating an enum class

Suppose that you have a class like this:

```
public class Chess {
  public static int LEFT=0;
  public static int RIGHT=1;
  public static int FORWARD=2;
  public static int BACKWARD=3;

  private int x, y;

  public void move(int direction) {
    switch (direction) {
      case LEFT:
        x--;
        break;
      case RIGHT:
        x++;
        break;
      case FORWARD:
        y++;
        break;
      case BACKWARD:
        y--;
        break;
    }
  }
}
```

However, this is not that good. For example, a caller may pass any integer to it:

```
Chess c = ...;
c.move(10);
```

To solve this problem, you can:

```
public enum Direction { LEFT, RIGHT, FORWARD, BACKWARD }
```

This is an "enum". An enum is basically a class. The class name here is "Direction".

```
public class Chess {
  private int x, y;

  public void move(Direction direction) {
    switch (direction) {
      case LEFT:
        x--;
        break;
      case RIGHT:
        x++;
        break;
      case FORWARD:
        y++;
        break;
      case BACKWARD:
        y--;
        break;
    }
  }
}
```

The compiler will translate the enum above into something like:

```
public class Direction {
  private String name;
  private int idx;

  private Direction(String name, int idx) {
    this.name = name;
    this.idx = idx;
  }
  public static Direction LEFT=new Direction("LEFT", 0);
  public static Direction RIGHT=new Direction("RIGHT", 1);
  public static Direction FORWARD=new Direction("FORWARD", 2);
  public static Direction BACKWARD=new Direction("BACKWARD", 3);
}
```

Now, it is error to pass it an int. You must pass a Direction object to it:

```
...
Chess c = ...;
c.move(10); //Compile error
c.move(Direction.LEFT); //OK
```

Note that the existing switch statement still works:

```
public enum Direction { LEFT, RIGHT, FORWARD, BACKWARD }

public class Chess {
  ...
  public void move(Direction direction) {
    switch (direction) {
      case LEFT:
        x--;
        break;
      ...
    }
  }
}
```

switch works for enum objects too, not just integrals.

Just write LEFT, not Direction.LEFT. From the switch expression the compiler knows the type is Direction, so it will look for the constants defined there.

An enum can be an inner class:

```
public class Chess {
  public enum Direction { LEFT, RIGHT, FORWARD, BACKWARD }
  ...
  public void move(Direction direction) {
    switch (direction) {
      case LEFT:
        x--;              It is automatically made a static class. By nature an
        break;            enum object should be self-contained and should not
        ...               refer to an outer object.
    }
  }
}
```

Converting between an enum value and a string

If you call toString() on an enum value, it will return its name. This allows you to print it easily:

```
public class Chess {
  public void move(Direction direction) {
    System.out.println("Moving to "+direction); //"Moving to LEFT"
    ...
  }
}
```

If you'd like to ask the user to input the direction (as a string), then you need to convert the string to an enum value. This can be done like this:

```
String s = "RIGHT";
Direction d = Direction.valueOf(s);
System.out.println(d == Direction.RIGHT); //Will print "True"
```

Comparing enum values

Each enum class is made to implement Comparable automatically and thus has a compareTo() method. You can use it like this:

```
Direction d1 = ...;
Direction d2 = ...;
if (d1.compareTo(d2) < 0) {
  ...
}
```

To see if two enum values are equal, you may use the equals() method. However, as there is no way to say create a new Direction value that equals to Direction.LEFT but is not Direction.LEFT, so if it equals to Direction.LEFT, it must be Direction.LEFT. It means that you can simply use the == operator to compare two enum values:

```
Direction d1 = ...;
Direction d2 = ...;
if (d1==d2) {
  ...
}
```

Iterating all the values in an enum

An enum class has a static method values() that will return an array of all the enum values in it (in the order of their appearance):

```
Chess c;
Direction[] dirs = Direction.values(); //{LEFT, RIGHT, FORWARD, BACKWARD}
for (Direction d: dirs) {
  if (c.canMove(d)) { //assuming Chess has a canMove() method
    ...
  }
}
```

Building a set of enum values

You can also create a Set from a range of enum values or from specific values:

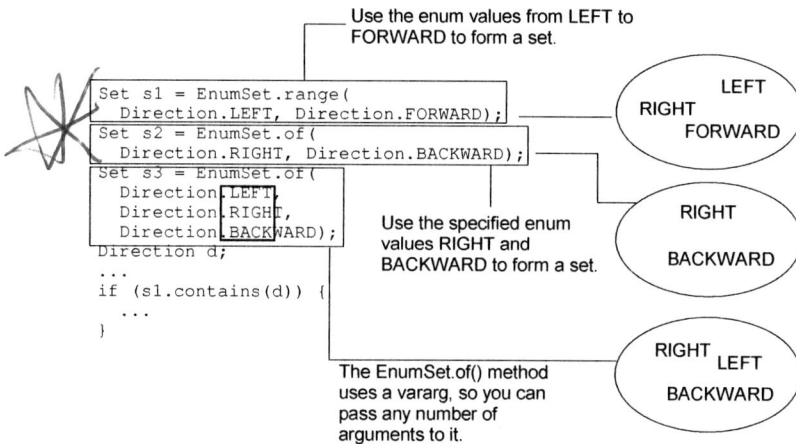

Use the enum values from LEFT to FORWARD to form a set.

```
Set s1 = EnumSet.range(
  Direction.LEFT, Direction.FORWARD);
Set s2 = EnumSet.of(
  Direction.RIGHT, Direction.BACKWARD);
Set s3 = EnumSet.of(
  Direction.LEFT,
  Direction.RIGHT,
  Direction.BACKWARD);
Direction d;
...
if (s1.contains(d)) {
  ...
}
```

LEFT
RIGHT
FORWARD

Use the specified enum values RIGHT and BACKWARD to form a set.

RIGHT
BACKWARD

The EnumSet.of() method uses a vararg, so you can pass any number of arguments to it.

RIGHT LEFT
BACKWARD

Note that the Sets have no ordering. In addition, the EnumSets are very efficient and can be used just like a bitmap of flags.

Adding data and behaviors to an enum

In addition to the idx and name automatically provided, you can add instance variables and methods to an enum class. For example:

```
public enum Direction {
  LEFT(-1, 0), RIGHT(1, 0), FORWARD(0, 1), BACKWARD(0, -1);

  private int deltaX;
  private int deltaY;

  private Direction(int deltaX, int deltaY) {
    this.deltaX = deltaX;
    this.deltaY = deltaY;
  }
  public void moveChess(Chess c) {
    c.setX(c.getX()+deltaX);
    c.setY(c.getY()+deltaY);
  }
}
...
public class Chess {
  public void move(Direction direction) {
    direction.moveChess(this);
  }
  ...
}
```

Provide arguments to the constructor

End with ";". After that, you can write it just like a normal class.

The constructor must be private!

Assuming Chess has the getters and setters

Call the method

If required, you can even define methods for each value:

```
public enum Direction {
  LEFT {
    public void moveChess(Chess c) {
      c.setX(c.getX()-1);
    }
  },
  RIGHT {
    public void moveChess(Chess c) {
      c.setX(c.getX()+1);
    }
  },
  FORWARD {
    public void moveChess(Chess c) {
      c.setY(c.getY()+1);
    }
  },
  BACKWARD {
    public void moveChess(Chess c) {
      c.setY(c.getY()-1);
    }
  };
  public abstract void moveChess(Chess c);
}
```

The compiler will create a sub-class for it:

Still use a comma to separate the enum values

```
public class Direction {
  ...
  public static Direction LEFT=
    new Direction("LEFT", 0) {
      public void moveChess(Chess c) {
        c.setX(c.getX()-1);
      }
    };
}
```

Still end with a semicolon

It doesn't have to be abstract. If not abstract, you need to provide a body here. Each anonymous subclass may override it.

Must declare the method here, otherwise no one can "see" this method.

The Enum base class

Each enum class you define will have instance variables such as idx and name and will have some methods such as toString(). There is no need to duplicate these in each enum class. Instead, Java provides a base class named "Enum" to provide these and automatically let your enum classes inherit from it. It is like:

```
public class Enum implements Comparable {
```

```
    private String name;
    private int idx;

    private Enum(String name, int idx) {
      this.name = name;
      this.idx = idx;
    }
    public String toString() {
      ...
    }
}
```

The Direction enum will be translated into:

```
public class Direction extends Enum {
  ...
}
```

However, the Comparable class is now generic, you need to specify a type:

```
interface Comparable<T> {
  int compareTo(T obj);
}
```

For the current case, you'd like something like:

```
public class Enum implements Comparable<Direction> {
  ...
  int compareTo(Direction obj) {
    ...
  }
}
public class Direction extends Enum {
  ...
}
```

However, the Enum class can never refer to your Direction class as it is pre-defined and must work with any enum that people define. So it should be a generic too:

```
public class Enum<T> implements Comparable<T> {
  ...
  int compareTo(T obj) {
    ...
  }
}
public class Direction extends Enum<Direction> {
  ...
}
```

However, the Enum class is accepting any type as T, so one may even use it like Enum<String> which doesn't make sense. T should be a type like the Direction class which extends Enum. So it should be:

```
public class Enum<T extends Enum> implements Comparable<T> {
  ...
  int compareTo(T obj) {
    ...
  }
}
public class Direction extends Enum<Direction> {
  ...
}
```

This is not entirely true though because Direction is extending Enum<Direction>, not the raw Enum. So the correct solution is:

```
public class Enum<T extends Enum<T>> implements Comparable<T> {
  ...
```

```
  int compareTo(T obj) {
    ...
  }
}
public class Direction extends Enum<Direction> {
  ...
}
```

Note that the SCJP exam doesn't require you to know the exact declaration of the Enum class. This is just an exercise to strengthen your understanding on generics.

Summary

An enum is a class with a list of pre-defined static values. No new values can be created. Each value has an index and a name. Their indexes are sequentially assigned from 0. Enum values can be compared to one another. You can convert between an enum value and a string. You can also get all the enum values in an enum or take some of them to form a Set to be used as a bitmap.

An enum always extends the Enum class.

You can add data and/or behaviors to your enum class or to each enum value. The latter is implemented using an anonymous class.

Review questions

3. Declare a Currency enum with the following values: USD, GBP, YEN, AUD, NZD, EUR.

4. The code below is trying to print the currencies. Fill in the blanks:

```
for (Currency c: _____) {
    System.out.println(_____);
}
```

5. Create a Set containing the high-interest currencies (AUD, NZD):

```
Set highInterestCurrencies = _____(Currency.AUD, Currency.NZD);
```

Answers to review questions

1. Declare a Currency enum with the following values: USD, GBP, YEN, AUD, NZD, EUR.

```
public enum Currency {
   USD, GBP, YEN, AUD, NZD, EUR
}
```

2. The code below is trying to print the currencies. Fill in the blanks:

```
for (Currency c: Currency.values()) {
   System.out.println(c);
}
```

3. Create a Set containing the high-interest currencies (AUD, NZD):

```
Set highInterestCurrencies = EnumSet.of(Currency.AUD, Currency.NZD);
```

Mock exam

2. Given the code below, how to get all the values in the enum?

```
11. enum Fruit {
12.    APPLE, ORANGE, PEAR, LEMON
13. }
```

a. new Fruit().getAll()

b. Fruit.all

c. Fruit.getEnumSet()

d. Fruit.values()

3. What is false about enums?

a. You can define fields in an enum class.

b. You can define methods in an enum class.

c. You can define methods for each enum value.

d. You create an enum value using the new operator.

4. What is true about the code below?

```
1.    enum Fruit {
2.       APPLE(10), ORANGE(13), PEAR(5), LEMON(20);
3.
4.       private int vitaminC;
5.
6.       public Fruit(int vitaminC) {
7.          this.vitaminC = vitaminC;
8.       }
9.       public int getVitaminC() {
10.         return vitaminC;
11.      }
12. }
```

a. There is a compile error at line 2.

b. There is a compile error at line 4.

c. There is a compile error at line 6.

d. There is a compile error at line 9.

e. It will compile fine.

5. What is true about the code below?

```
1.    public enum Foo {
2.       FooA {
3.          public String g() {
4.             return "hello";
5.          }
6.       },
7.       FooB;
8.
9.       public String g() {
10.         return toString();
11.      }
```

```
12.    public static void main(String[] args) {
13.      System.out.println(FooA.g());
14.      System.out.println(FooB.g());
15.    }
16. }
```

a. It will print "FooA" and then "FooB".

b. It will print "hello" and then "FooB".

c. It will print "hello" and then "hello".

d. It won't compile.

Answers to the mock exam

1. d.

2. d. As the constructor is private, you can't use the new operator to create an enum object. You're forced to use the constants.

3. c. The constructor must be private.

4. b. FooA has overridden the g() method to return "hello". For FooB, it will use the g() method in Foo, which will return the name of FooB ("FooB").

Chapter 7

Static Imports

What's in this chapter?

In this chapter you'll learn how to use static imports.

Static imports

Suppose that you have a class Foo:

```
package app1;

public class Foo {
  public static String NAME = "abc";
  public static void g(int i) {

    ...
  }
}
```

If you'd like to use its static variables or static methods in another class, you can do it this way:

```
package app2;

import app1.Foo;

public class Bar {
  private void g2() {
    String s = Foo.NAME;
    Foo.g(2);
    Foo.g(4);
    Foo.g(5);
  }
}
```

If you need to call g() very frequently, it is tedious to keep writing "Foo." each time. To solve this problem, you can:

```
package app2;
                            ┌──── import the g() method in
  import app1.Foo;          │     Foo
  import static app1.Foo.g;

  public class Bar {
    private void g2() {
      String s = Foo.NAME;
      g(2);        Now you can call the g()
      g(4);        method without writing
      g(5);        "Foo."
    }
  }
```

If you'd like, you can import the NAME static variable too:

```
package app2;       ┌──── This line is no longer needed as Foo is
                    │     not used in the code
  import app1.Foo;
  import static app1.Foo.g;        ┌──── import the NAME variable
  import static app1.Foo.NAME;

  public class Bar {
    private void g2() {
      String s = NAME;      Now you can use the
      g(2);                 NAME variable without
      g(4);                 writing "Foo."
      g(5);
    }
  }
```

If you'd like, you can import all static members (variables and methods) in Foo:

```
package app2;

import static app1.Foo.*;         import all static
                                   members of Foo

public class Bar {
    private void g2() {            Use the NAME variable
        String s = NAME;           without writing "Foo."
        g(2);
        g(4);                      Call the g() method without
        g(5);                      writing "Foo."
    }
}
```

Static imports and enums

Static imports work very well with enums. For example:

```
package app1;

public enum Currency {
    USD, GBP, AUD
}

package app2;

import static app1.Currency.*;

public class Foo {
    void g() {
        Set s = EnumSet.of(USD, AUD); //No need to write Currency.USD
        ...
    }
}
```

Summary

Static imports allow you to import the static members of a class.

Review questions

4. Given the code:

```
package x.y;

public class Foo {
  public static final int ABC=10;
  public static void g() {
  }
}
```

You'd like to use Foo in a class in another package. Fill out the table for each case:

Requirement	Import statement
Import ABC	
Import g()	
Import all static members of Foo	

Answers to review questions

1. Given the code:

```
package x.y;

public class Foo {
  public static final int ABC=10;
  public static void g() {
  }
}
```

You'd like to use Foo in a class in another package. Fill out the table for each case:

Requirement	Import statement
Import ABC	import static x.y.Foo.ABC
Import g()	import static x.y.Foo.g
Import all static members of Foo	import static x.y.Foo.*

Mock exam

5. Fill in the blank to import the DEFAULT_VALUE:

```
17. package com.foo;
18.
19. public class Foo {
20.    public static final int DEFAULT_VALUE = 10;
21. }
22.
23. package com.bar;
24.
25. _____;
26.
27. public class Bar {
28. }
```

a. import com.foo.Foo.DEFAULT_VALUE

b. import static com.foo.Foo.DEFAULT_VALUE

c. static import com.foo.Foo.DEFAULT_VALUE

d. static import com.foo.Foo

Answers to the mock exam

1. b.

Chapter 8

Covariant Return Types

What's in this chapter?

In this chapter you'll learn about a change to the rule of overriding methods in Java: covariant return types.

Narrowing the return type

In J2SE 1.4 or earlier, if you override a method, the return type must remain unchanged:

```
class Foo {
  Foo copy() {
    ...
  }
}
class Bar extends Foo {
  Foo copy() {
    ...
  }
}
```

This results in awkward code like:

```
Bar b1 = new Bar();
Bar b2 = (Bar)b1.copy(); //must type cast
```

In JSE 5, you can narrow the return type to its subclass, e.g., from Foo to Bar:

```
class Foo {
  Foo copy() {
    ...
  }
}
class Bar extends Foo {
  Bar copy() {
    ...
  }
}
```

This will allow much cleaner code:

```
Bar b1 = new Bar();
Bar b2 = b1.copy(); //do not need to type cast
```

What about the clients of Foo such as:

```
Foo f1 = ...;
Foo f2 = f1.copy();
```

As the clients are prepared to handle any Foo object as the return, returning a Bar object won't break them as a Bar object is also a Foo object.

As you're changing the type to Bar in the Bar class, i.e., the return type is changing along with the class, this is called "covariant return type". This is the most common usage, but it is not a requirement. For example, you may write:

```
class Foo {
  InputStream open() {
    ...
  }
}
class Bar extends Foo {
  BufferedInputStream open() {
```

```
    ...
  }
}
```

Note that this works when the return type is a class. It doesn't work if it is a primitive type:

```
class Foo {
  long g() {
    ...
  }
}
class Bar extends Foo {
  int g() { //Compile error
    ...
  }
}
```

This is because no one is going to convert the int to a long. The g() in Bar is not going to do that because the client may be using Bar and expecting an int, not a long. The client of Foo is not going to do it because it is expecting a long, not expecting an int.

In addition, while you can make the return type narrower, you can't make the parameter types wider:

```
class Foo {
  void g(Foo f) {
    ...
  }
}
class Bar extends Foo {
  void g(Object f) { //You're overloading it, not overriding it.
    ...
  }
}
```

The only exception is when you're overriding a generic version using its erasure.

Summary

When overriding a method, you can make its return type narrower if it is a class.

Review questions

2. Will the following code compile?

```
class Foo {
  Number getSize() {
    ...
  }
}
class Bar extends Foo {
  Integer getSize() {
    ...
  }
}
```

3. Will the following code compile?

```
class Foo {
  Integer getSize() {
    ...
  }
}
class Bar extends Foo {
  Number getSize() {
    ...
  }
}
```

4. Will the following code compile?

```
class Foo {
  double getSize() {
    ...
  }
}
class Bar extends Foo {
  float getSize() {
    ...
  }
}
```

Answers to review questions

1. Will the following code compile?

```
class Foo {
  Number getSize() {
    ...
  }
}
class Bar extends Foo {
  Integer getSize() {
    ...
  }
}
```

Yes. Integer is a subclass of Number.

2. Will the following code compile?

```
class Foo {
  Integer getSize() {
    ...
  }
}
class Bar extends Foo {
  Number getSize() {
    ...
  }
}
```

No. You can't make the return type wider. This will break the clients of Foo.

3. Will the following code compile?

```
class Foo {
  double getSize() {
    ...
  }
}
class Bar extends Foo {
  float getSize() {
    ...
  }
}
```

No. You can't change the return type if it is a primitive type.

Mock exam

2. What is true about the following code?

```
29. interface Parser {
30.   Object parse(Reader r);
31. }
32. class CommandParser implements Parser {
33.   public Command parse(Reader r) {
34.     ...
35.   }
36. }
37. class Command {
38.   ...
39. }
```

a. There is a compile error at line 5.

b. There is an unchecked warning at line 5.

c. There is a compile error at line 9. To fix it, you need to explicitly write "Command extends Object".

d. It will compile fine.

3. What is true about the following code?

```
1.  class Foo {
2.    List makeList() {
3.      return new ArrayList();
4.    }
5.  }
6.  class Bar extends Foo {
7.    List<String> makeList() {
8.      return new ArrayList<String>();
9.    }
10. }
```

a. There is a compile error at line 7.

b. There is an unchecked warning at line 7.

c. It will compile fine.

d. It will throw a runtime exception at line 8.

Answers to the mock exam

1. c. Implementing a method is a form of overriding. So you can narrow the return from Object to Command.

2. d. List<String> is a subclass of List. So this is allowed.

Chapter 9

Java I/O

What's in this chapter?

In this chapter you'll learn how to perform I/O.

Using the File class

The java.io.File class represents a file system path. For example:

```
File f1 = new File("c:\\d1\\f1");//On Windows. Use \\ to mean \ in a string
File f2 = new File("/usr/local/f2"); //On Unix
```

Note that you can create such File objects even though the files do NOT exist. To check if a file does exist, do something like:

```
File f = new File("c:\\d1\\f1");
if (f.exists()) {
  ...;
}
```

If the file does exist, it may be a normal file or a directory. If it is a directory, you can list the files (including sub-directories) in it:

```
File f = new File("c:\\d1\\f1");
if (f.isDirectory()) {
  File[] children = f.listFiles();
  ...
}
if (f.isFile()) {
  ...
}
```

If you like, you can create a File object from its parent directory and its name:

```
File d1 = new File("c:\\d1");
File f1 = new File(d1, "f1"); //The same path (c:\d1\f1)
```

You can also create a File object from a relative path:

```
File f1 = new File("f1"); //f1 in the current directory
```

If the File is a normal file, you can get its size (in bytes), which is a long value:

```
File f = new File("c:\\d1\\f1");
long size = f.length();
```

You can delete a file or a directory:

```
File f = new File("c:\\d1\\f1");
f.delete();
```

You can create a directory:

```
File d = new File("c:\\d1\\d2");
d.mkdir();
```

Note that you can NOT read or write the file content using the File class. To do that, you need to use some other classes.

InputStream

An InputStream (in the java.io package) is a sequence of bytes. You can read the bytes sequentially. For example, if there is an InputStream that represents a sequence of 4, 57, -2, 127, you can read the bytes. However, the bytes are returned as int values in the range of 0-255. So, in this case, you will get 4, 57, 254, 127 respectively. If you try to read one more byte, it will return -1 to mean that you have reached the end:

```
InputStream in = ...;
int b1 = in.read(); //b1 is 4
int b2 = in.read(); //b2 is 57
int b3 = in.read(); //b3 is 254
int b4 = in.read(); //b4 is 127
int b5 = in.read(); //b5 is -1
```

You can also try to read multiple bytes into a byte array:

```
InputStream in = ...;
byte[] buf = new byte[10];
int r1 = in.read(buf);
int r2 = in.read(buf);
```

r1 is the actual number of bytes read. It is possible that it may not read all the 4 bytes due to buffering. It will read at least 1 byte (may be 1, 2, 3 or 4 bytes). If it does read all the bytes (4 bytes), then when you read it again, it will return -1 (r2 in the code above).

After using an InputStream, you should close it to release the resources it allocated:

```
InputStream in = ...;
in.read();
...
in.close();
```

The InputStream class is abstract. So, you can't create an instance directly. It has some subclasses. For example, there is a FileInputStream class so you can read the bytes in a given file:

```
InputStream in = new FileInputStream("c:\\f1");
...
in.close();
```

Here you use a string to represent the path. You can also use a File object instead:

```
File f = new File("c:\\f1");
InputStream in = new FileInputStream(f);
...
in.close();
```

If the file f1 doesn't exist, the constructor will throw a FileNotFoundException. If there are any errors reading the bytes, it will throw an IOException.

OutputStream

Note that you can read the bytes from an InputStream, but you can't write to it. To write some bytes out, you need to use an OutputStream (also in the java.io package). Just like an InputStream, it is an abstract class and you need to use a subclass. For example, to write to a file, you can use a FileOutputStream:

```
OutputStream out = new FileOutputStream("c:\\f1"); //create f1 if required
out.write(10);
out.write(255);
byte[] buf = new byte[] {1, 3, 5};
```

```
out.write(buf); //write 3 bytes, otherwise it will throw an exception
out.close();
```
If there is any error writing the bytes, it will throw an IOException.

Reading and writing primitive values

You can write bytes to an OutputStream, but you can't write say an int, a long, a double, a boolean or a string to an OutputStream. They must be converted to bytes first. This can be done with a DataOutputStream (in the java.io package) which performs this conversion. For example, it will convert an int into four bytes:

```
DataOutputStream out = new DataOutputStream(
  new FileOutputStream("c:\\f1"));
out.writeDouble(32.0d);
out.writeInt(255);
out.writeUTF("hello");
out.close();
```
Note that you need to give it an OutputStream to its constructor. When you tell it to write say a double, it will convert it into 8 bytes (in a platform independent way. That is, no matter it is running on Windows or Linux, the same double value will be converted into the same 8 bytes). Then it will write the bytes to that OutputStream. You don't need to close that OutputStream. When you close the DataOutputStream, it will close the OutputStream automatically.

To read the data back, you use a DataInputStream:

```
DataInputStream in = new DataInputStream(new FileInputStream("c:\\f1"));
double d = in.readDouble(); //32.0
int i = in.readInt(); //255
String s = in.readUTF(); //"hello"
in.close();
```

Reading and writing strings

How to convert a non-English char such as '你' into bytes? It depends on what encoding you use. For example, if you use BIG5, '你' might be converted into two bytes 139 and 26. If using UTF-8, it might be converted into three bytes 192, 81 and 234.

If you write a string using the writeUTF() method in the DataOutputStream class, the string is converted into bytes using an encoding similar to UTF-8. However, sometimes you'd like to use some other encodings such as BIG5. In that case, you should use a Writer (in the java.io package):

```
Writer writer = new OutputStreamWriter(
  new FileOutputStream("c:\\f1"), "BIG5");
writer.write("hello"); //will be encoded into bytes using BIG5
writer.close();
```
Again, you pass an OutputStream to the constructor so that it will write the bytes there. The desired encoding is also passed to the constructor.

To read back the strings, use a Reader (also in the java.io package):

```
Reader reader = new InputStreamReader(
  new FileInputStream("c:\\f1"), "BIG5");
int r;
while ((r = reader.read()) != -1) { //-1 means no more
        char c = (char)r; //should be 'h', then 'e', 'l', 'l' and 'o'.
  ...
}
reader.close();
```

To write strings to a file, Java provides a convenient sub-class of Writer, FileWriter:

```
Writer writer = new FileWriter("c:\\f1");
writer.write("hello");
writer.close();
```

However, using this class, you can't specify the encoding; it always uses the default encoding of the system (e.g., for Traditional Chinese Windows, it's Big5). Similarly, you can use a FileReader:

```
Reader reader = new FileReader("c:\\f1");
...
reader.close();
```

Buffered reading/writing

If you use a normal OutputStream or a normal Writer, each time you write a single byte or a single character to it, it will write it immediately. This may be slow if you have many bytes or characters to write. To speed it up, it may buffer the bytes or characters. When the buffer is full, it can write the whole buffer out in one go. This buffering function is provided by BufferedOutputStream and BufferedWriter (also in the java.io package):

```
Writer writer = new BufferedWriter(new FileWriter("c:\\f1"));
writer.write("hello"); //this may be buffered
writer.write("world"); //this may also be buffered
...
writer.close();
```

Again, you need to pass a Writer to its constructor. When you writes some data to it, it will write the data to its buffer. When the buffer is full, it will write data to that Writer and empty the buffer. If you'd like to force it to write the data even though the buffer is not full, you can call flush():

```
//must declare it as a BufferedWriter in order to call flush() because
//the Writer class doesn't have this method.
BufferedWriter writer = new BufferedWriter(new FileWriter("c:\\f1"));
writer.write("hello");
writer.write("world");
writer.flush();
...
writer.close();
```

In any case, close() will flush the data automatically.

It is similar for BufferedOutputStream:

```
OutputStream out = new BufferedOutputStream(
  new FileOutputStream("c:\\f1"));
out.write(23);
...
out.close();
```

Similarly, to speed up reading, you can use a BufferedReader or a

BufferedInputStream:

```
BufferedReader reader = new BufferedReader(new FileReader("c:\\f1"));
int ch = reader.read();
String line = reader.readLine();
reader.close();
```

The BufferedReader class has a readLine() method which is not in the Reader class. It reads all the characters until it finds a newline. It will read that newline but it is not included in the string returned. On end of file, it will return null.

Reading and writing primitive data as text strings

You can use a Writer to write strings, but what if you'd like to output an int value say 23 as a string "23"? You could convert it into a string first and then write the string to a Writer, but Java provides a convenient subclass of Writer that can do this for you: PrintWriter.

```
PrintWriter writer = new PrintWriter(new FileWriter("c:\\f1"));
writer.print(23); //Will output "23"
writer.print(true); //Will output "true"
writer.println(2.3); //Will output "2.3\n"
writer.close();
```

Reading and writing objects

You can easily write out a whole object using the ObjectOutputStream class :

```
class Foo implements Serializable {
  private int i;
  private String s;
}
...
Foo foo1 = new Foo();
Foo foo2 = new Foo();
ObjectOutputStream out = new ObjectOutputStream(
  new FileOutputStream("c:\\f1"));
out.writeObject(foo1);
out.writeObject(foo2);
out.close();
```

The writeObject() method will check if the class being output implements the Serializable interface or not. If not, it will throw a NotSerializableException. The Serializable interface defines no method at all. It is there so that you can indicate that the class is intended to be serialized. If it does implement Serializable, the writeObject() method will write the class name and the field values to the OutputStream. The fields don't have to be public nor to have getters. This process is called "serialization".

To read the objects back:

```
ObjectInputStream in = new ObjectInputStream(
  new FileInputStream("c:\\f1"));
Foo foo1 = (Foo)in.readObject();
Foo foo2 = (Foo)in.readObject();
in.close();
```

The readObject() method will read the class name, then create an instance of that class, read the field values and set them. Because it uses a very low level method to create the instance, your Foo class doesn't need to have a no-argument constructor nor setters for the fields.

Many Java built-in classes such as List, Set, Map, String, Date do implement Serializable, so you can write them into an ObjectOutputStream.

If you'd like to exclude a certain field from serialization, you can mark it as transient:

```
class Foo implements Serializable {
  private int i;
  transient private String s;
}
```

If a Foo object refers to some other objects or even arrays of other objects, those objects will also be serialized:

```
class Foo implements Serializable {
  private int i;
  private String s;
  private Bar bar;
  private Object[] objs;
}
class Bar implements Serializable {
  ...
}
```

Note that the Bar class and the class of each object in "objs" must implement Serializable, otherwise a NotSerializableException will be thrown. If a Bar object refers to some other objects, they will also be serialized. That is, a whole object graph may be serialized in a single call to writeObject(). If an object appears twice in the graph, only one copy will be saved. For example, if O1 refers to O2 and O2 refers to O1, when dealing with the O1 referred to by O2, only the reference to O1 will be saved, not O1 itself and therefore no looping will occur.

If you'd like to decide how to write out the field values, you can do it this way:

```
class Foo implements Serializable {
  private int i;
  private String s;

  private void writeObject(ObjectOutputStream out)
    throws IOException {
    out.writeInt(i);
    out.writeUTF(s);
  }
  private void readObject(ObjectInputStream in)
    throws IOException, ClassNotFoundException {
    i = in.readInt();
    s = in.readUTF();
  }
}
```

Note that even though an ObjectOutputStream extends OutputStream but not DataOutputStream, it does have the same methods as those in DataOutputStream such as writeInt(), writeUTF() and etc.

If Foo extends a class that already implements Serializable, it doesn't need to implement Serializable again:

```
class Base implements Serializable {
  private int n;
}
```

```
class Foo extends Base {
  private int i;
  private String s;
}
```

If the Base class doesn't implement Serializable but you'd like Foo to, Foo should implement writeObject() and readObject() to handle the fields in the Base (the "n" here), otherwise those fields will simply be ignored:

```
class Base {
  private int n;

  public int getN() {
    return n;
  }
  public void setN(int n) {
    this.n = n;
  }
}
class Foo extends Base implements Serializable {
  private int i;
  private String s;

  private void writeObject(ObjectOutputStream out)
    throws IOException {
    out.writeInt(getN());
    out.defaultWriteObject(); //work on the current obj
  }
  private void readObject(ObjectInputStream in)
    throws IOException, ClassNotFoundException {
    setN(in.readInt());
    in.defaultReadObject(); //work on the current obj
  }
}
```

In addition, Base needs to have a no-argument constructor accessible to Foo. When reading a Foo object back, the instance will be created and then such a constructor will be called to initialize the fields in Base, before the fields in Foo are set.

In summary, if the inheritance relationship is C1, C2, C3 and C4 (C1 is the ancestor) and you're serializing a C4 object, if C1 and C2 are not implementing Serializable but C3 does, then C4 doesn't need to do that and its fields will be included, but C2 needs to have a no-argument constructor accessible to C4 (so that it can initialize the fields in C1 and C2) and C3 needs to define writeObject() and readObject() to serialize and deserialize the fields in C1 and C2.

Versioning in object serialization

Suppose that you've stored a Foo object into a file. Later you add some fields to the Foo class. When you try to read that Foo object back, Java will find that the class has changed and will throw an Exception. But in principle this can still be made to work because it could simply not set the new fields (or you could read it in your readObject() method). To suppress the error, before you store the Foo object into the file, you need to assign a version # to the Foo class:

```
class Foo implements Serializable {
```

```
private static final long serialVersionUID = 1L;
...
}
```

When you add new fields to it, do NOT change this version #. This way readObject() will find that the version in the file and the version in the JVM are the same and thus will go ahead. If you don't specify a version #, writeObject() will calculate a version # based on the class itself and readObject() will do the same calculation. If some fields are added, the calculated version # will change.

If you remove fields from the Foo class and thus prevent the deserialization of the object, you should change (e.g., increment) the version #. This will protect yourself when someone tries to read an old Foo object back.

Summary

The File class represents a file system path. It doesn't mean the file exists. It can be used to check the existence of the file, get its size, make a directory, delete a file/directory, list the content of a directory and etc.

To read and write bytes, use InputStream/OutputStream. To read and write primitive values, use DataInputStream/DataOutputStream. To read and write text, use Reader/Writer. To write primitive values as text, use PrintWriter. To use buffering on streams, use BufferedInputStream/BufferedOutputStream. To use buffering on readers, use BufferedReader/BufferedWriter.

To read from files, use FileInputStream (bytes) or FileReader (text in the default encoding). To read text in a non-default encoding, use an InputStreamReader along with a FileInputStream. To write to files, use FileOutputStream (bytes) or FileWriter (text in the default encoding). To write text in a non-default encoding, use an OutputStreamWriter along with a FileOutputStream.

To read and write objects, use an ObjectInputStream/ObjectOutputStream. Make sure the class directly implements Serializable or inherits it from an ancestor. In the inheritance chain the first class that directly implements Serializable needs access to the no-argument constructor in its parent and it should save and load the fields in its ancestors in its readObject() and writeObject() methods. Its subclasses don't need to do anything to support object serialization.

Review questions

4. Will the code below create the file c:\f1?

```
File f = new File("c:\\f1");
```

5. List the methods of the File class:

Purpose	Method
Delete the file	
Delete the directory	
Create it as a directory	
Get the file size	
Check if the file exists	
Check if it is a regular file	
Check if it is a directory	

6. You'd like to calculate the sum of all the bytes in the file c:\f1. Fill in the blanks:

```
File f = new File("c:\\f1");
InputStream in = new _____(f);
int b;
int sum = 0;
for (;;) {
    b = in._____();
    if (b==____) {
        break;
    }
    sum += b;
}
in._____();
```

7. The above code is inefficient because it reads each byte without any buffering. In order to use buffering, what should you do?

```
File f = new File("c:\\f1");
InputStream in = new _____(new _____(f));
...
```

8. You'd like to write some primitive values into c:\f1 as binary data. What should you do?

```
_____ out = new _____(
    new FileOutputStream("c:\\f1"));
out.writeDouble(32.0d);
out.writeInt(255);
out.writeDouble(53.7d);
out.close();
```

9. In the code above, how many bytes would be output?

10. Write code to read the data back:

```
_____ in = new _____(new FileInputStream("c:\\f1"));
double d1 = in._____();
int i = in._____();
double d2 = in._____();
```

```
in._____();
```

11. You'd like to write some text into c:\f1 using the BIG5 encoding. What should you do?

```
Writer writer = new _____(
   new _____("c:\\f1"), _____);
writer.write("hello");
writer.close();
```

12. If you'd like to print primitive values as strings, which class should you use?

13. You'd like to serialize some Foo objects into c:\f1, what should you do?

```
class Foo implements _____ {
  private int i;
  private String s;
}
...
_____ out = new _____(
   new _____("c:\\f1"));
out._____(new Foo());
out._____(new Foo());
out.close();
```

14. In the code above, do you need to have getters for "i" and "s"? Do you need a no-argument constructor in Foo?

15. If you'd like to exclude the "i" field in the Foo class above from serialization, what should you do?

16. If you'd like to control how the fields of the Foo class above are serialized, what should you do?

17. For the code below, if you'd like to serialize Foo objects, does it need to implement Serializable?

```
class Base implements Serializable {
  private int n;
}
class Foo extends Base {
  private int i;
  private String s;
}
```

Answers to review questions

1. Will the code below create the file c:\f1?

```
File f = new File("c:\\f1");
```

No. A File object is only a path. The file may or may not exist.

2. List the methods of the File class:

Purpose	Method
Delete the file	delete()
Delete the directory	rmdir()
Create it as a directory	mkdir()
Get the file size	length()
Check if the file exists	exists()
Check if it is a regular file	isFile()
Check if it is a directory	isDirectory()

3. You'd like to calculate the sum of all the bytes in the file c:\f1. Fill in the blanks:

```
File f = new File("c:\\f1");
InputStream in = new FileInputStream(f);
int b;
int sum = 0;
for (;;) {
  b = in.read();
  if (b==-1) {
    break;
  }
  sum += b;
}
in.close();
```

4. The above code is inefficient because it reads each byte without any buffering. In order to use buffering, what should you do?

```
File f = new File("c:\\f1");
InputStream in = new BufferedInputStream(new FileInputStream(f));
...
```

5. You'd like to write some primitive values into c:\f1 as binary data. What should you do?

```
DataOutputStream out = new DataOutputStream(
  new FileOutputStream("c:\\f1"));
out.writeDouble(32.0d);
out.writeInt(255);
out.writeDouble(53.7d);
out.close();
```

6. In the code above, how many bytes would be output?

20. A double takes 64 bits (8 bytes). An int takes 32 bits (4 bytes). As there are two doubles and one int, the total is 2*8+4=20 bytes.

7. Write code to read the data back:

```
DataInputStream in = new DataInputStream(new FileInputStream("c:\\f1"));
double d1 = in.readDouble();
int i = in.readInt();
double d2 = in.readDouble();
in.close();
```

8. You'd like to write some text into c:\f1 using the BIG5 encoding. What should you do?

```
Writer writer = new OutputStreamWriter(
  new FileOutputStream("c:\\f1"), "Big5");
writer.write("hello");
writer.close();
```

9. If you'd like to print primitive values as strings, which class should you use?

PrintWriter.

10. You'd like to serialize some Foo objects into c:\f1, what should you do?

```
class Foo implements Serializable {
  private int i;
  private String s;
}
...
ObjectOutputStream out = new ObjectOutputStream(
  new FileOutputStream("c:\\f1"));
out.writeObject(new Foo());
out.writeObject(new Foo());
out.close();
```

11. In the code above, do you need to have getters for "i" and "s"? Do you need a no-argument constructor in Foo?

No.

12. If you'd like to exclude the "i" field in the Foo class above from serialization, what should you do?

Mark it as transient.

13. If you'd like to control how the fields of the Foo class above are serialized, what should you do?

Define the readObject() and writeObject() methods.

14. For the code below, if you'd like to serialize Foo objects, does it need to implement Serializable?

```
class Base implements Serializable {
  private int n;
}
class Foo extends Base {
  private int i;
  private String s;
}
```

No.

Mock exam

3. In order to read the bytes in a file, which class should you use?

   a. File

   b. FileInputStream

   c. FileOutputStream

   d. FileReader

4. In order to delete a file, which class should you use?

   a. File

   b. FileInputStream

   c. FileOutputStream

   d. FileWriter

5. Suppose that the InputStream "in" is representing a file that contains 1000 bytes. What is the value of n?

```
11. byte[] buf = new byte[512];
12. int n = in.read(buf);
13. System.out.println(n);
```

   a. 511

   b. 512

   c. It could be any value between 1 and 512.

   d. It could be -1 or 512.

6. In the code above, what happens if there is an error when reading from an InputStream at line 2?

   a. It will return -1

   b. It will return 0

   c. It will throw an IOException

   d. It will throw an IOError

7. What method you should call on an InputStream to release the resources occupied by it?

   a. close()

   b. release()

  c. free()

  d. This is done automatically.

8. In order to read a text file line by line, which two classes do you need? (Choose 2)

  a. FileReader

  b. FileInputStream

  c. BufferedReader

  d. BufferedInputStream

  e. DataInputStream

9. In order to read a text file in a non-default encoding, which class do you need?

  a. TextInputStream

  b. FileReader

  c. InputStreamReader

  d. BufferedReader

  e. DataReader

10. You would like to save Foo objects into a file using object serialization, what does the Foo class have to do?

  a. Implement the serializeObject() method properly.

  b. Implement the writeObject() method properly.

  c. Implement the Serializable interface.

  d. Nothing. This function is provided by the ObjectOutputStream class.

11. What methods are declared in the Serializable interface?

  a. Nothing.

  b. writeObject() and readObject().

  c. serializeObject() and deserializeObject().

  d. save() and load().

12. In order to output the text representation of int values and double values into a file, which class should you use?

a. DataOutputStream

b. DataWriter

c. PrintOutputStream

d. PrintWriter

Answers to the mock exam

1. b. File represents a path, not file content. FileReader can be used to read text, not bytes.

2. a.

3. c. It will read at least 1 byte. It will never read more than the buffer can hold.

4. c. -1 is used to indicate EOF, not error.

5. a.

6. a and c. To read text line by line, you need a BufferedReader, which in turn needs a Reader. To read from a file, that should be a FileReader.

7. c. To read text, you need a Reader. FileReader always use the default encoding so it is incorrect. BufferedReader simply uses another Reader so there is no way to specify the encoding. InputStreamReader is correct because you can specify the encoding.

8. c.

9. a. Serializable is only a marker interface. It contains nothing.

10. d.

Chapter 10

Formatting and Parsing

What's in this chapter?

In this chapter you'll learn how to perform formatting and parsing using the API in Java.

Locale

A locale contains a language code and optionally a country code. For example:

Locale	Meaning
en	English
en_US	English in US
en_UK	English in UK
zh	Chinese
zh_CN	Chinese in PRC
zh_TW	Chinese in Taiwan
fr_FR	French in France
fr_CA	French in Canada

The idea is that, in different locales, people use different languages, different formats to represent a date, different formats to represent a currency and etc. Your program may support two or more locales. For each user, you can check his locale and display messages in his language, display dates in that locale's format and etc.

The default locale of the JVM is the locale of the user who started the JVM. The locale of the user is set in the OS (e.g., in Windows, it is set in Control Panel | Regional Settings). If this is not what he wants, he can set the default locale for the JVM when launching it:

```
java -Duser.language=en -Duser.country=US ...
```

You can get the default locale using:

```
Locale def = Locale.getDefault();
```

You can create Locale objects in your program like this:

```
Locale locale1 = new Locale("en"); //just the language code
Locale locale2 = new Locale("en", "US"); //language code & country code
```

The Locale class has defined some commonly used locale objects that can be used directly:

```
class Locale {
    public static final Locale ENGLISH = new Locale("en");
    public static final Locale US = new Locale("en", "US");
    public static final Locale CHINESE = new Locale("zh");
    public static final Locale CHINA = new Locale("zh", "CN");
```

```
    public static final Locale TAIWAN = new Locale("zh", "TW");
    public static final Locale FRENCH = new Locale("fr");
}
```

Formatting and parsing numbers

It may seem easy to convert an int say 1234 into a string. However, when you consider showing a thousand separator, it will be more difficult because in some countries (locales) a comma is the separator while in others a dot is used:

```
Some countries: 1,234
Some others: 1.234
```

Fortunately, Java provides a class to do that: java.text.NumberFormat. Use it like this:

```
NumberFormat f = NumberFormat.getInstance(Locale.US);
String s;
s = f.format(1234); //s is "1,234"
f = NumberFormat.getInstance(Locale.GERMANY);
s = f.format(1234); //s is "1.234"
```

The locale is optional. If you don't specify it, then the default locale in the system is used:

```
NumberFormat f = NumberFormat.getInstance();
f.format(123);
```

You can format an int as a currency (to get dollar signs and etc.):

```
NumberFormat f = NumberFormat.getCurrencyInstance(Locale.US);
f.format(1234); //$1,234.00
f = NumberFormat.getCurrencyInstance(Locale.GERMANY);
f.format(1234); //1.234,00 €
f = NumberFormat.getCurrencyInstance(); //default locale
f.format(1234); //depend on your system
```

NumberFormat is an abstract class, so you can't create instances from it directly. The getXXXInstance() methods will automatically find a suitable subclass to create the instance.

You can use a NumberFormat to parse a number from a string:

```
NumberFormat f = NumberFormat.getCurrencyInstance(Locale.US);
Number n = f.parse("$1,234.00");
int i = n.intValue(); //1234
double d = n.doubleValue(); //1234d
```

If the default format (for each locale) is not what you want, you can specify a format pattern. Here is a typical format pattern:

At least 4 integer digits. Pad with zeros as needed.

3 optional fractional digits. That is, at most 7 fractional digits. If there are 8 digits, it will be rounded. If there are just 6 digits, only 6 digits will be displayed.

```
0000.0000###
```

At least 4 fractional digits. Pad with zeros as needed.

Note that there is no maximum limit on the number of integer digits. That is, a large number will never be cut short. In addition, you can specify a prefix, a suffix and a thousands separator:

The prefix is a string and will be displayed as is

The suffix is a string and will be displayed as is

```
USD0,000.0000###XYZ
```

Display a thousands separator (for that locale) for every 3 integer digits

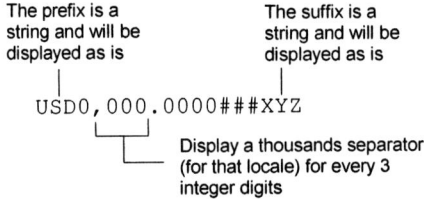

Here are some examples:

Index	Pattern	Meaning	Examples
1	0.0#	At least one integer digit (but could be more), then a decimal point (localized), then at least one fractional digit (if none, show as 0), then another optional fractional digit. If there are more digits, it is rounded. Note that there is no limit on the maximum number of integer digits.	0.344 => "0.34" 120 => "120.0"
2	#,##0.0#	Same as pattern 1 except that it uses a thousands separator (localized) for every 3 integer digits (i.e., grouping size is 3).	1234.5 => "1,234.5"
3	,##0.0#	Same as pattern 2. The # at the beginning is not really needed.	
4	##,#0.0#	Same as pattern 2 except that the grouping for every 2 integer digits, not 3.	1234.5 => "12,34.5"
5	#	No fractional digits	0.344 => "0" 120 => "120"
6	0000	At least 4 integer digits and no fractional digits	0.344 => "0000" 120 => "0120"
7	0.0#; (0.0#)	Two patterns are provided and separated by a semi-colon. The first is for positive numbers and the second is for negative numbers. The parentheses here are simply output as is and have no special meaning at all.	1.2 => "1.2" -1.2 => "(1.2)"
8	0.0#;(#)	Actually in the second pattern only the prefix (if any) and suffix (if any) are used. The grouping size, minimum number of digits and etc. will use those from the first pattern. So, this pattern is exactly the same as pattern 7.	

To specify a format pattern, do it this way:

```
NumberFormat f = NumberFormat.getInstance();
//can set the pattern only if it is a DecimalFormat. This should be
//true for most cases.
if (f instanceof DecimalFormat) {
  DecimalFormat df = (DecimalFormat) f;
  df.applyPattern("0.0#");
}
f.format(1234.567); //1234.57
```

Note that the maximum and minimum number of digits above are used for formatting only; they don't affect parsing at all.

Formatting and parsing dates

To format a Date into a string, use the java.text.DateFormat class:

```
Date d = new GregorianCalendar(2006, 0, 20).getTime();
DateFormat f = DateFormat.getDateInstance(DateFormat.SHORT, Locale.US);
f.format(d); //"1/20/06"
f = DateFormat.getDateInstance(DateFormat.MEDIUM, Locale.US);
f.format(d); //"Jan 20, 2006"
f = DateFormat.getDateInstance(DateFormat.LONG, Locale.US);
f.format(d); //"January 20, 2006"
f = DateFormat.getDateInstance(DateFormat.FULL, Locale.US);
f.format(d); //"Friday, January 20, 2006"
```

The exact meaning of a style depends on the locale. The locale also affects the pattern, the names of the months and etc.:

Style	English	Germany
SHORT	1/20/06	20.01.06
MEDIUM	Jan 20, 2006	20.01.2006
LONG	January 20, 2006	20. Januar 2006
FULL	Friday, January 20, 2006	Freitag, 20. Januar 2006

If you don't specify the locale, the default system locale will be used:

```
DateFormat f = DateFormat.getDateInstance(DateFormat.SHORT);
...
```

If you don't specify the style, the default style for the default locale will be used:

```
DateFormat f = DateFormat.getDateInstance();
...
```

You can use a DateFormat for parsing:

```
DateFormat f = DateFormat.getDateInstance(DateFormat.SHORT, Locale.US);
Date d = f.parse("1/20/06");
```

You can also format times or date-times:

```
Date d = new GregorianCalendar(2006, 0, 20, 9, 30, 20).getTime();
DateFormat f1 = DateFormat.getTimeInstance(DateFormat.SHORT, Locale.US);
f1.format(d); //"9:30 AM"
//For date-time, specify two styles: one for the date, one for the time.
DateFormat f2 = DateFormat.getDateTimeInstance(
```

```
DateFormat.SHORT, DateFormat.SHORT, Locale.US);
f2.format(d); //"1/20/06 9:30 AM"
```

If the default format pattern (for each locale) is not what you want, you can specify a format pattern. Here are some example patterns:

Index	Pattern	Meaning	Examples
1	yyyy-MM-dd	"y" means year. "yyyy" means a minimum of four characters. The hyphen is output as is. "M" means month. "MM" means a minimum of two characters. "d" means day in month. "dd" means a minimum of two characters.	2006-01-20 2006-12-20
2	yyyy-MMM-dd	When there are 3 or more "M", the month will be displayed as a localized month name (a text string). If there are 4 or more letters in a text string pattern, the full version is used ("January"), otherwise a shorthand will be used ("Jan").	2006-Jan-20
3	yyyy-MMMM-dd	Use full version of month names	2006-January-20
4	yyyy-M-dd	Same as pattern 1 except that the minimum number of characters is 1 for the month.	2006-1-20 2006-12-20
5	yy-MM-d	When there are exactly 2 "y", it will truncate the year to 2 characters (2006 displayed as "06"). Note that truncation will NOT happen with others such as "M" or "d". When parsing, "06" should be 2006, 1906 or 2106? It depends on the date when the DateFormat object is created. Suppose that it is 2000, then it will assume the year is in the range of year 1920 (2000-80) to 2020 (2000+20). So, it will treat "06" as 2006. If the input string is "80", then it will be treated as 1980.	06-01-20 06-01-4
6	yy-MM-dd E	The space is displayed as is. "E" means day in the week (string). Just like another other string patterns, if there were 4 or more "E", full version would be used. Now the shorthand will be used.	06-01-20 Fri
7	yy-MM-dd EEEE	Use full version of the day in the week.	06-01-20 Friday

To specify a Date pattern, do it this way:

```
Date d = new GregorianCalendar(2006, 0, 20, 9, 30, 20).getTime();
DateFormat f = DateFormat.getDateInstance();
//can set the pattern only if it is a SimpleDateFormat. This should be
//true for most cases.
if (f instanceof SimpleDateFormat) {
        SimpleDateFormat sdf = (SimpleDateFormat) f;
        sdf.applyPattern("yyyy-MM-dd");
}
f.format(d); //"2006-01-20"
```

Note that the minimum number of characters above affect formatting only; it doesn't affect parsing at all. For text strings, both the full version and the shorthand will be accepted regardless of the number of characters in the pattern (No matter you're using "E" or "EEEE").

Formatting several values

You can format several values into a single string using the MessageFormat class (see below). The format() method will format each element in the Object array. In this case the return value will be the string "I have 123 on Jan 20, 2006". In the pattern string, {0} means the 0th argument and {1} means the 1st argument. If you don't specify the locale, it will use the default of the system.

```
Date d = new GregorianCalendar(2006, 0, 20, 9, 30, 20).getTime();
MessageFormat f = new MessageFormat("I have {0} on {1}", Locale.US);
String s = f.format(
    new Object[] {        The 0th argument
        new Integer(123),
        d });
                    The 1st argument
```

For each argument, you can further specify its type and style:

```
Date d = new GregorianCalendar(2006, 0, 20, 9, 30, 20).getTime();
MessageFormat f = new MessageFormat(
    "I have {0,number,currency} and {1,date,full}");
String s = f.format(
    new Object []
        new Integer(123),              Use the FULL
        d });                          style
    Use a NumberFormat   Call
    to format the 0th    getCurrencyInstance()
    argument             on the NumberFormat   Use a DateFormat to
                         to get the instance   format the 1st
                                                argument
```

To have greater control, you may also specify a pattern for each argument:

```
MessageFormat f = new MessageFormat(
    "I have {0,number,0.00#} and {1,date,yyyy-MMM-dd}");
```

Formatter

There is another way to format values: the Formatter class in the java.util package. It is like the printf() function in C/C++:

The formatted output will be stored into this StringBuffer

The Locale is not used here. It will be used if say it needs to output a thousands separator or a month name.

```
StringBuffer sb = new StringBuffer();
Formatter f = new Formatter(sb, Locale.US);
f.format("Hello %d %s", new Integer(1234), "abc");
System.out.println(sb.toString());
```

"Hello" and the space following it are displayed as is

It is a "format specifier". It will format the next argument (1234) as a decimal.

Another format specifier. It will format the next argument ("abc") as a string. If it is not a String, it will call toString() on the argument.

In this example, the output will be "Hello 1234 abc".

You can specify which argument to format using its index. Use 1$ to mean the first argument, 2$ to mean the second and etc.:

```
f.format("Hello %1$d %2$s %1$d", new Integer(1234), "abc");

Result:
Hello 1234 abc 1234
```

Note that it is 1-based, not 0-based as in MessageFormat.

You can specify the argument index for some format specifiers and not specify it for some others. For those not having an argument index, they will get the arguments sequentially:

```
f.format("%1$d %d %s", new Integer(1234), "abc");
//%1$d => first argument
//%d => get next argument (first argument)
//%s => get next argument (second argument)

Result:
1234 1234 abc
```

You can specify the minimum number of characters to output (called the "width"). For example, if the width is 6 and the original output is "1234", two extra spaces will be added to the beginning and the output will be " 1234":

```
//specify a "width" of 6
f.format("%6d %s", new Integer(1234), "abc");

Result:
  1234 abc
```

The width can also be applied to %s such as:

```
f.format("%d %5s", new Integer(1234), "abc");

Result:
1234   abc
```

You can specify the maximum number of characters to output (called the "precision"). This works for %s, but not for %d because it doesn't make sense to cut off an integer:

```
//set the "precision" to 7
f.format("Hello %d %5.7s", new Integer(1234), "abcdefghi");

Result:
Hello 1234 abcdefg
```

You can output using floating point formats:

```
f.format("%1$f %1$e %1$g", new Double(1234.56));
//%f => floating point format
//%e => scientific format
//%g => general format

Result:
1234.560000 1.234560e+03 1234.56
```

You can also specify the width and the precision. The width still means the minimum number of characters in the output (including the decimal point if any). For %f and %e, the precision now refers to the maximum number of fractional digits. For %g, the precision now refers to the maximum number of all digits:

```
f.format("%8.1f", new Double(1234.56));
f.format("%8.1g", new Double(1234.56));
f.format("%8.4g", new Double(1234.56));

Result:
  1234.6 //at most 1 fractional digit
   1e+03 //at most 1 digit (the exponent is not counted)
    1235 //at most 4 digits
```

Instead of using spaces to pad, you can ask it to pad using zeros. This works only for numbers, not for strings (because it just doesn't make sense to pad zeros to a string):

```
//add a "0" before the width. This is called a "flag".
f.format("%08.1f %05d", new Double(1234.56), new Integer(1234));

Result:
001234.6 01234
```

Instead of padding zeros or spaces to the beginning, you can ask it to pad spaces to the end (so it is left-aligned):

```
//use a "-" flag.
f.format("%-8.1f %-5d", new Double(1234.56), new Integer(1234));

Result:
1234.6   1234
```

There is no way to pad zeros to the end and it just doesn't make sense (will change the value). So, don't try to use both flags together (%-08d or %-08d).

To output a date:

```
Date d = new GregorianCalendar(2006, 0, 20, 9, 30, 20).getTime();
f.format("%1$tY %1$ty %1$tB %1$tb %1$tm %1$td", d);
//%tY => year in four digits
//%ty => year in two digits
//%tB => full month name (localized)
//%tb => shorthand month name (localized)
//%tm => month as a number
//%td => day in month

Result:
2006 06 January Jan 01 20
```

You can specify the width, but you can't specify a precision. You can also use the "-" flag (but not the "0" flag).

You can output the whole date in some common formats:

```
Date d = new GregorianCalendar(2006, 0, 20, 9, 30, 20).getTime();
f.format("%1$tD %1$tF %1$tT", d);
//%tD => mm/dd/yy
```

```
//%tF => yyyy-mm-dd
//%tT => hh:mm:ss

Result:
01/20/06 2006-01-20 09:30:20
```

You can output a newline (\n on Unix; \r\n on Windows):

```
f.format("Hello%nWorld");
//%n => newline

Result:
Hello
World
```

Because a % has special meaning in the format string, how to output a % itself? Just use two %'s:

```
f.format("%%");

Result:
%
```

You can send formatted output to System.out easily:

```
System.out.printf("%d %s", new Integer(123), "abc");
System.out.format("%d %s", new Integer(123), "abc"); //exactly the same
```

Internally it will create a Formatter object to format the output before sending the output to itself. Similarly, the String class also provides this function through a static method:

```
String result = String.format("%d %s", new Integer(123), "abc");
...
```

Using regular expressions

Suppose that a car license number must start with the character "X" and then followed by any 3 characters. Now given a string, how to check if it represents a valid license number? You can do it this way:

The Pattern and Matcher classes are located in this package

It means we're expecting an "X" by any three characters. A dot means any character. Such a pattern is called a "regular expression".

```
import java.util.regex.*;
...
String s = "X123";
Pattern pattern = Pattern.compile("X...");
Matcher matcher = pattern.matcher(s);
if (matcher.matches()) {
    System.out.println("Matched!");
}
```

This creates a "Matcher". The matcher will try to match the regular expression against the string s.

A Pattern object is just a regular expression that has been compiled for efficiency.

Try to match the pattern against the whole string

Actually, the regular expression above can be simplified:

```
...
Pattern pattern = Pattern.compile("X.{3}");
...
```

{3} means to repeat the previous item (the dot) three times

Here are some other common regular expressions:

Regular expression	Meaning
a?	"?" means the previous item is optional. In this case, it means there is 0 or 1 "a".
a+	"+" means there are 1 or more occurrences of the previous item. In this case, one or more "a".
a*	"*" means there are 0 or more occurrences of the previous item. In this case, 0 or more "a".
.	"." means any single character.
[a-g]	A single character from "a" to "g".
[a-zA-Z]	A single character from "a" to "z" or from "A" to "Z". That is, an alphabet.
[^a-zA-Z]	A single character that is not an alphabet.
[0-9]	A digit.
\d	A digit.
\d{8}	8 digits
\d{6,8}	6 to 8 digits
\d{6,}	6 or more digits
a|b	"a" or "b"
(ab)|(cd)	"ab" or "cd".
ab|cd	"a", followed by "b" or "c", then followed by "d".
\?	A "?" character. Backslash can remove the special meaning of the following item. Here the "?" loses its special meaning (optional) and only means a question mark itself.
\+	A "+" character.
\.	A "." character.
\(	A "(" character.
\\	A "\" character. Here the first backslash is removing the special meaning of the second backslash.
\s	A space character, i.e., a space, tab, newline, return, linefeed
\w	A word character, i.e., a-z, A-Z, 0-9 and underscore.

Here are some examples:

Requirements	Regular expression	Extra explanation
A local phone # which consists of 8 digits.	\d{8}	
A phone # that have an optional country code. The country code is 1-3 digits enclosed in parentheses if it is present.	(\(\d{1,3}\))?\d{8}	The outer () is used to group the country code so that it can be marked as optional. The inner () is escaped to mean parentheses.
A Java identifier.	[a-zA-Z_$][a-zA-Z_$0-9]*	
A Java identifier.	[a-zA-Z_$][\w$]*	
An integer that may have a sign.	[+-]?\d+	

Note that to have a "\" in a Java string, you need to write "\\":

```
String s = "(123)12345678";
Pattern pattern = Pattern.compile("(\\(\\d{1,3}\\))?\\d{8}");
Matcher matcher = pattern.matcher(s);
if (matcher.matches()) {
        System.out.println("Matched!");
}
```

You don't have to match the whole string. You may match a part of a string:

```
String s = "123ab4c5";
Pattern pattern = Pattern.compile("[a-z]+");
Matcher matcher = pattern.matcher(s);
if (matcher.find()) {
    System.out.println(matcher.start());
    System.out.println(matcher.end());
    System.out.println(matcher.group());
}
if (matcher.find()) {
    System.out.println(matcher.start());
    System.out.println(matcher.end());
    System.out.println(matcher.group());
}
if (matcher.find()) {
    ...
}
```

Try to match a part of the string. Here it will match "ab". So it will return true. You can find out which part was matched by querying the matcher:

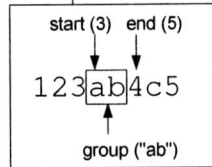

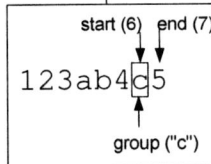

start (3) end (5)

123ab4c5

group ("ab")

It will return false because there is no more match

start (6) end (7)

123ab4c5

group ("c")

To allow you to perform whole-string matching easily, the Pattern class provides a convenient method:

```
class Pattern {
  static boolean matches(String pattern, String s) {
    Pattern p = Pattern.compile(pattern);
```

```
        Matcher matcher = p.matcher(s);
        return matcher.matches();
    }
}
```

You can use it like this:

```
String s = "(1)12345678";
if (Pattern.matches("(\\(\\d{1,3}\\))?\\d{8}", s)) {
        System.out.println("Matched!");
}
```

Note that if you have a pattern and you'll match it against multiple strings, for better performance you should create a Pattern object first and then use it to match multiple strings. This way the compilation is only done once.

The String class also provides a similar matches() method:

```
class String {
  boolean matches(String pattern) {
    return Pattern.matches(pattern, this);
  }
}
```

You can use it like this:

```
String s = "(1)12345678";
if (s.matches("(\\(\\d{1,3}\\))?\\d{8}")) {
        System.out.println("Matched!");
}
```

If you'd like to split a string "a,b,c" using the comma as the separator, you can do it this way:

```
Pattern pattern = Pattern.compile(",");  //"," is a regular expression
String s = "a,b,c";
String[] strings = pattern.split(s);
System.out.println(strings[0]); //"a"
System.out.println(strings[1]); //"b"
System.out.println(strings[2]); //"c"
```

There is no static split() method in Pattern class, but there is a split() method in the String class:

```
String s = "a,b,c";
String[] strings = s.split(","); //Pass it a regular expression
System.out.println(strings[0]); //"a"
System.out.println(strings[1]); //"b"
System.out.println(strings[2]); //"c"
```

Again, if you need to use the same separator to split multiple strings, creating the Pattern object first is more efficient.

What happens if you try to split "a,b,c" using a hyphen as the separator? As the separator is the not found, the string is not split and the whole string is returned as the sole element in the string array:

```
String s = "a,b,c";
String[] strings = s.split("-");
System.out.println(strings[0]); //"a,b,c"
```

Instead of splitting a string, you can also replace the matches using another string:

```
String s = "a,b,c";
s = s.replaceAll(",", "-"); //s is now "a-b-c"
```

Parsing text data

Suppose that you have a text file containing information about bank accounts. Each account has an id, the owner's name and a balance:

```
acc001,Kent,1000,acc002,Paul,1500,...
```

How to read data from the file? You can use the Scanner class in the java.util package:

```
Scanner scanner = new Scanner("c:\\f1", "BIG5");
scanner.useDelimiter(","); //this is a regular expression
while (scanner.hasNext()) {
        String accNo = scanner.next();
        String ownerName = scanner.next();
        int balance = scanner.nextInt();
        ...
}
scanner.close();
```

If the file is like:

```
acc001,Kent,1000
acc002,Paul,1500
...
```

Then, you will need to parse it line by line. In this case, the delimiter is not used:

```
Scanner scanner = new Scanner("c:\\f1", "BIG5");
while (true) {
    String string = scanner.findInLine("(\\w*),(\\w*),(\\d+)");
    if (string == null) {
        break;
    }
    MatchResult result = scanner.match();
    String accNo = result.group(1);
    String ownerName = result.group(2);
    int balance = Integer.parseInt(result.group(3));
    ...
    if (scanner.hasNextLine())
        scanner.nextLine();
    } else {
        break;
    }
}
scanner.close();
```

try to match the regular expression against the input, but never go beyond a newline char.

null means no match

get the part matching the 1st ()

get the part matching the 2nd ()

get the part matching the 3rd ()

after the match, is there a newline char in the rest of the input?

skip the newline char & go to the start of the next line

A Scanner doesn't have to read from a text file. It can read from a string, a Reader or an InputStream:

```
Scanner scanner1 = new Scanner("acc001,Kent,1000,acc002,Paul,1500,...");
Reader r = ...;
Scanner scanner2 = new Scanner(r);
InputStream in = ...;
Scanner scanner3 = new Scanner(in, "BIG5");
```

Summary

A locale is a token representing a convention to display numbers, currencies, dates, times and etc. In Java, it is specified by a language code and optionally country code.

To format a number as a number or a currency, ask NumberFormat for a suitable instance for the desired locale. You can specify a pattern if it is a DecimalFormat. Similarly, to format a date, a time or a date and time, use DateFormat. You can specify a pattern if it is a SimpleDateFormat. Both the NumberFormat and DateFormat support parsing.

To format many values in a sentence, use the MessageFormat class. To format many values in an aligned format, use the Formatter class or System.out.printf(), System.out.format() or String.format().

You can use a regular expression to match a whole string, parts of a string or to split a string. For this, you can use the Pattern and the Matcher classes. The String class also provides convenient methods for matching a whole string or splitting a string.

To parse information from a stream or a file token by token, use the Scanner class. You can get each token by specifying a delimiter (a regular expression). If the input is line by line, you can specify a regular expression to extract the information while limiting it to the current line.

Review questions

15. A Locale contains a _____ and optionally a _____.

16. How to create a Locale for Chinese in Taiwan?

```
Locale l = new Locale(____, ____);
```

17. How to create a NumberFormat for French?

```
NumberFormat f = _____;
```

18. How to create a NumberFormat to format currency for French?

```
NumberFormat f = _____;
```

19. What DecimalFormat pattern to use for each case?

Requirements	Pattern
At least 2 integer digits. At least 1 and at most 3 fractional digits. No thousands separator.	
At least 2 integer digits. At least 1 and at most 3 fractional digits. Show thousands separator.	
No minimum number of integer digits. No minimum number of fractional digits and at most 4 fractional digits. No thousands separator.	
Same as above but negative numbers are shown in parentheses.	
At least 5 integer digits and no fractional digits. No thousands separator.	

20. How to create a long style DateFormat (for date displays) for French and a default style for the default locale respectively?

```
DateFormat f1 = _____;
DateFormat f2 = _____;
```

21. How to create a long style DateFormat (for time displays) for French and a default style for the default locale respectively?

```
DateFormat f1 = _____;
DateFormat f2 = _____;
```

22. What SimpleDateFormat pattern to use for each case?

Samples	Pattern
2006/02/05	
06/02/05	
2006-Feb-05	
2006-February-05	
2006/2/5	

Samples	Pattern
2006/2/5 Mon	
2006/2/5 Monday	

23. Fill in the blanks below to output a message like "My account balance is $1,000 on 2006/01/20". It should use the default currency format and the short style date format for default locale.

```
Date today = new Date();
int balance = 1000;
MessageFormat f = new MessageFormat(_____);
String s = f.format(_____);
```

24. What format specifier (for the Formatter class) to use for each case?

Requirements	Format specifier
Format the 2nd argument as a string.	
Format the next argument as a decimal. If the output is less than 6 characters, pad spaces at the beginning.	
Format the next argument as a decimal. If the output is less than 6 characters, pad spaces at the end.	
Format the next argument as a decimal. If the output is less than 6 characters, pad zeros at the beginning.	
Format the 1st argument as in general format. If the output is less than 6 characters, pad spaces at the beginning.	
Format the 1st argument as in floating point format. If the output is less than 8 characters, pad spaces at the beginning. Round it if there are more than 3 fractional digits.	
Format the next argument as a 4-digit year.	
Format the next argument as a 2-digit year.	
Format the next argument as a month.	
Format the next argument as a shorthand month name.	
Format the next argument as a full month name.	
Format the next argument as a day in month.	
Output a newline	
Output a %	

25. Write the regular expression for each case:

Requirements	Regular expression
An alphabet, followed by 4 digits.	
One or more alphabets. The first alphabet is in capital case.	
An English word, i.e., one or more alphabets.	
A sentence. One or more English words (consisting of word characters), separated by a space character (including tab and etc.).	
A 4-digit year or a 2-digit year.	
A floating point number without any sign, i.e., zero or more digits, followed by a decimal point and one or more digits.	

26. Given a string s = "abc def ghi", you call _____ to extract the substrings "abc", "def" and "ghi".

27. You'd like to extract the data from a string. Fill in the blanks:

```
String s = "abc,123,def,222,...";
Scanner scanner = new Scanner(_____);
scanner.useDelimiter(_____);
while (scanner._____()) {
        String x = scanner._____();
        int i = scanner._____();
        ...
}
scanner._____();
```

Answers to review questions

1. A Locale contains a <u>language code</u> and optionally a <u>country code</u>.

2. How to create a Locale for Chinese in Taiwan?

```
Locale l = new Locale("zh", "TW");
```

3. How to create a NumberFormat for French?

```
NumberFormat f = NumberFormat.getInstance(Locale.FRENCH);
```

4. How to create a NumberFormat to format currency for French?

```
NumberFormat f = NumberFormat.getCurrencyInstance(Locale.FRENCH);
```

5. What DecimalFormat pattern to use for each case?

Requirements	Pattern
At least 2 integer digits. At least 1 and at most 3 fractional digits. No thousands separator.	00.0##
At least 2 integer digits. At least 1 and at most 3 fractional digits. Show thousands separator.	,#00.0##
No minimum number of integer digits. No minimum number of fractional digits and at most 4 fractional digits. No thousands separator.	.####
Same as above but negative numbers are shown in parentheses.	.####;(#)
At least 5 integer digits and no fractional digits. No thousands separator.	00000

6. How to create a long style DateFormat (for date displays) for French and a default style for the default locale respectively?

```
DateFormat f1 = DateFormat.getDateInstance(DateFormat.LONG, Locale.FRENCH);
DateFormat f2 = DateFormat.getDateInstance();
```

7. How to create a long style DateFormat (for time displays) for French and a default style for the default locale respectively?

```
DateFormat f1 = DateFormat.getTimeInstance(DateFormat.LONG, Locale.FRENCH);
DateFormat f2 = DateFormat.getTimeInstance();
```

8. What SimpleDateFormat pattern to use for each case?

Samples	Pattern
2006/02/05	yyyy/MM/dd
06/02/05	yy/MM/dd
2006-Feb-05	yyyy-MMM-dd
2006-February-05	yyyy-MMMM-dd
2006/2/5	yyyy/M/d

Samples	Pattern
2006/2/5 Mon	yyyy/M/d E
2006/2/5 Monday	yyyy/M/d EEEE

9. Fill in the blanks below to output a message like "My account balance is $1,000 on 2006/01/20". It should use the default currency format and the short style date format for default locale.

```
Date today = new Date();
int balance = 1000;
MessageFormat f = new MessageFormat("My account balance is
{0,number,currency} on {1,date,short}");
String s = f.format(new Object[]{new Integer(balance), today});
```

10. What format specifier (for the Formatter class) to use for each case?

Requirements	Format specifier
Format the 2nd argument as a string.	%2$s
Format the next argument as a decimal. If the output is less than 6 characters, pad spaces at the beginning.	%6d
Format the next argument as a decimal. If the output is less than 6 characters, pad spaces at the end.	%-6d
Format the next argument as a decimal. If the output is less than 6 characters, pad zeros at the beginning.	%06d
Format the 1st argument as in general format. If the output is less than 6 characters, pad spaces at the beginning.	%1$6g
Format the 1st argument as in floating point format. If the output is less than 8 characters, pad spaces at the beginning. Round it if there are more than 3 fractional digits.	%1$8.3f
Format the next argument as a 4-digit year.	%tY
Format the next argument as a 2-digit year.	%ty
Format the next argument as a month.	%tm
Format the next argument as a shorthand month name.	%tb
Format the next argument as a full month name.	%tB
Format the next argument as a day in month.	%td
Output a newline	%n
Output a %	%%

11. Write the regular expression for each case:

Requirements	Regular expression
An alphabet, followed by 4 digits.	[a-zA-Z]\d{4}
One or more alphabets. The first alphabet is in capital case.	[A-Z][a-zA-Z]*
An English word, i.e., one or more alphabets.	[a-zA-Z]+
A sentence. One or more English words (consisting of word characters), separated by a space character (including tab and etc.).	\w+(\s\w+)*
A 4-digit year or a 2-digit year.	\d{4}|\d{2}
A floating point number without any sign, i.e., zero or more digits, followed by a decimal point and one or more digits.	\d*\.\d+

12. Given a string s = "abc def ghi", you call <u>s.split(" ")</u> to extract the substrings "abc", "def" and "ghi".

13. You'd like to extract the data from a string. Fill in the blanks:

```
String s = "abc,123,def,222,...";
Scanner scanner = new Scanner(s);
scanner.useDelimiter(",");
while (scanner.hasNext()) {
        String x = scanner.next();
        int i = scanner.nextInt();
        ...
}
scanner.close();
```

Mock exam

11. What is a major advantage of using the NumberFormat class to format currencies?

    a. It is very efficient because it is implemented in a native method.

    b. It supports the scientific notation so that very large quantities can be formatted.

    c. It will use locale-specific symbols.

    d. It can be customized by overriding some of its methods.

12. How should you create a NumberFormat instance to format a number?

```
14. NumberFormat f = _____;
15. f.format(123.456);
```

    a. new NumberFormat()

    b. new DecimalFormat()

    c. NumberFormat.getInstance()

    d. NumberFormat.getCurrencyInstance()

13. Which DecimalFormat pattern should you use to get results like 1234.5 => "1,234.50"?

    a. ####.00

    b. ,###.00

    c. ,###.0#

    d. ,###.##

14. How should you create a DateFormat instance to format a time?

```
1.   DateFormat f = _____;
2.   f.format(...);
```

    a. new DateFormat()

    b. new SimpleDateFormat()

    c. new TimeFormat()

    d. DateFormat.getTimeInstance()

15. Which is NOT a style supported by DateFormat?

    a. DateFormat.BRIEF

    b. DateFormat.MEDIUM

    c. DateFormat.LONG

    d. DateFormat.FULL

16. Which SimpleDateFormat pattern should you use to get results like "2006/November/28"?

    a. YYYY/M/dd

    b. yyyy/MM/d

    c. YY/MMM/dd

    d. yyyy/MMMM/d

17. In order to get results like below (the first row is the header to show you the columns), what format specifier to use with the Formatter?

```
01234567890123456 7890
  1234.50
    678.91
    356.25
```

    a. %8.2f

    b. %9.2f

    c. %-8.2f

    d. %9.2s

18. In order to get results like below (the first row is the header to show you the columns), what format specifier to use with the Formatter?

```
012345678901234567890
abc
abcdef
xyzxyz
```

    a. %6s

    b. %-6s

    c. %06s

    d. %06g

19. How to specify that a particular format specifier should be applied to the 2nd argument so that it is formatted as a decimal integer?

    a. %2$d

    b. %2$i

    c. %$2d

    d. %$2i

20. Suppose an email address takes the form <user>@<domain 1>.<domain 2>...<domain N> where N >= 2. That is, there are at least two domain name components. The <user> and <domain> parts contain one or more word characters (alphabets, digits and underscores). What is the regular expression for an email address?

    a. \w+@\w+(.\w+)+

b. \w*@\w*(.\w*)*

c. \w+@\w+(\.\w+)+

d. \w*@\w*(\.\w*)*

Answers to the mock exam

1. c.

2. c.

3. b. The pattern should have a minimum of 2 fractional digits and a thousands separator.

4. d.

5. a.

6. d. To get the full month name, you need at least 4 M's. A single d will not limit the day to 1 character. It is only the minimum, not the maximum.

7. b. It is a floating point format. The width is 9. The precision is 2. Spaces are padded at the beginning.

8. b. It is a string format. the width is 6. Spaces are padded at the end.

9. a.

10. c.

    a. The dot is not escaped, so it is interpreted as any character, not a dot in an email.

    b. The dot is not escaped. It also allows the user name or a domain to be empty.

    c. This is the correct answer.

    d. It allows the user name or a domain to be empty.

Chapter 11

Preparing for the Exam

Exam format

The Sun Certified Programmer for J2SE 5.0 Upgrade exam (CX-310-056) contains 46 questions. You need to answer 58% (27 questions) correctly in 105 minutes in order to pass.

Most questions are multiple choice questions with a single correct answer. In that case, each answer is represented by a radio button:

Q1: Which code fragment can be filled in to make the code below compile?

```
class Foo {
    public static void main(String[] args)
        throws InterruptedException {
        Thread t = new Thread(new Runnable() {
            public void run() {
                System.out.println("abc");
            }
        });
        t.start();
        _____;
        System.out.println("def");
    }
}
```

- ● t.join()
- ○ t.wait()
- ○ Thread.sleep(1000)
- ○ t.resume()

Some questions have more than one correct answers. In that case, each answer is represented by a check box (see the example below). Fortunately, the question will tell you exactly how many answers are correct.

Q1: Which code fragments can be filled in to make the code below compile? Choose 2.

```
import java.util.*;

class Foo<      > {
    T x;

    int g(T y) {
        return x.compareTo(y);
    }
}
```

- ☐ T extends Comparable<T>
- ☐ T implements Comparable<T>
- ☐ ? extends Comparable
- ☐ T extends Date

Some questions are drag-and-drop questions. Typically you are asked to drag the correct code into the right places (see the example below). Note that a code fragment may be used multiple times or none at all.

Q1: Drag the code into the right places so that it prints each line of a text file f1 and releases the resources properly.

```
_____ __ = new _____("f1");
_____ __ = new _____(s1);
while (true) {
    String line = __._____();
    if (line == null) {
        break;
    }
}
__._____();
```

```
  s1          s2          read        FileInputStream     FileReader

BufferedReader      readLine        free          close
```

Exam syllabus

The exam syllabus can be found at http://www.sun.com/training/catalog/courses/CX-310-056.xml. Note that it covers not only the Java SE 5 new features, but also important points in the 1.4 exam such as threading, overriding, overloading, access modifiers, constructors, common exceptions, classpath and etc. So, if you're using this book to prepare for the exam, make sure you still remember the important points in the 1.4 exam!

Freely available mock exams on the Internet

- http://www.javabeat.net/javabeat/scjp5/mocks/index.php

- http://www.javablackbelt.com

- More are listed at http://faq.javaranch.com/view?ScjpFaq#mocks

References

- Sun Microsystems. The Java Language Specification, Third Edition. http://java.sun.com/docs/books/jls.

- Sun Microsystems. The JDK™ 5.0 Documentation. http://java.sun.com/j2se/1.5.0/docs.

- Sun Microsystems. The Java™ Tutorials. http://java.sun.com/docs/books/tutorial.

- Angelika Langer. Java Generics FAQ. http://www.angelikalanger.com/GenericsFAQ/JavaGenericsFAQ.html.

Printed in the United Kingdom
by Lightning Source UK Ltd.
119589UK00003B/156